50 Summer Sweets Recipes for Home

By: Kelly Johnson

Table of Contents

- Fresh Berry Parfait
- Mango Sorbet
- Peach Cobbler
- Strawberry Shortcake
- Lemon Blueberry Cheesecake Bars
- Watermelon Mint Salad
- Coconut Lime Popsicles
- Grilled Pineapple with Honey Glaze
- Raspberry Lemonade Cupcakes
- Key Lime Pie
- Blackberry Lemon Sorbet
- Orange Creamsicle Smoothie
- Mixed Berry Crisp
- Kiwi Strawberry Popsicles
- Pineapple Upside-Down Cake
- Blueberry Lemon Scones
- Mint Chocolate Chip Ice Cream
- Cherry Almond Galette
- Honeydew Basil Sorbet
- Peach Melba
- Raspberry Swirl Cheesecake
- Lemon Poppy Seed Muffins
- Chocolate-Dipped Strawberries
- Vanilla Bean Ice Cream
- Caramelized Banana Split
- Pomegranate Granita
- Coconut Mango Rice Pudding
- Blueberry Lemonade Slushie
- Grilled Peaches with Cinnamon Sugar
- Strawberry Rhubarb Pie
- Mint Chocolate Brownie Bites
- Honey Lavender Ice Cream
- Raspberry Chocolate Tart
- Orange Creamsicle Cheesecake
- Berry Chia Seed Pudding

- Watermelon Sorbet
- Mango Coconut Popsicles
- Lemon Raspberry Swirl Pound Cake
- Peach and Raspberry Crumble
- Strawberry Basil Lemonade
- Blueberry Pancake Stack with Maple Syrup
- Coconut Pineapple Cake
- Cherry Chocolate Chip Ice Cream Sandwiches
- Lemon Thyme Shortbread Cookies
- Raspberry Almond Tart
- Peach Bellini Pops
- Blueberry Cheesecake Ice Cream
- Orange Creamsicle Cupcakes
- Mint Chocolate Mousse
- Vanilla Berry Popsicles

Fresh Berry Parfait

Ingredients:

    2 cups mixed fresh berries (strawberries, blueberries, raspberries, blackberries)
    1 cup Greek yogurt
    1/4 cup honey
    1 teaspoon vanilla extract
    1 cup granola

Instructions:

    Prepare Berries:
- Wash and dry the fresh berries thoroughly.
- If using strawberries, hull and slice them.

    Prepare Yogurt Mixture:
- In a bowl, mix the Greek yogurt, honey, and vanilla extract until well combined.

    Assemble Parfaits:
- In serving glasses or bowls, start with a layer of the Greek yogurt mixture.

    Add Berries:
- Add a generous layer of mixed fresh berries on top of the yogurt.

    Repeat Layers:
- Repeat the layers until the glasses are filled, finishing with a layer of berries on top.

    Top with Granola:
- Sprinkle granola over the final layer of berries to add a delightful crunch.

    Serve Immediately:
- Serve the fresh berry parfait immediately to enjoy the contrast of creamy yogurt, juicy berries, and crunchy granola.

Variations:

- For a tropical twist, add diced mango or pineapple to the berry mix.
- Drizzle a bit of melted dark chocolate between the layers for an indulgent touch.
- Experiment with flavored yogurts, such as vanilla, strawberry, or honey, to enhance the parfait's taste.

This Fresh Berry Parfait is a refreshing and visually appealing summer sweet that combines the natural sweetness of fresh berries with the creamy texture of Greek yogurt and the crunchiness of granola. Perfect for a light and satisfying dessert on a warm summer day!

Mango Sorbet

Ingredients:

- 4 cups ripe mango, peeled, pitted, and diced
- 1 cup granulated sugar
- 1 cup water
- 1/4 cup fresh lime or lemon juice
- Zest of one lime or lemon (optional)

Instructions:

Prepare Simple Syrup:
- In a small saucepan, combine sugar and water over medium heat. Stir until the sugar completely dissolves. Remove from heat and let it cool to room temperature to create a simple syrup.

Blend Mangoes:
- In a blender, puree the diced mango until smooth. You can leave some small mango chunks for texture if desired.

Combine Ingredients:
- In a bowl, mix the mango puree with the simple syrup, fresh lime or lemon juice, and optional zest. Stir well to ensure all ingredients are evenly combined.

Chill Mixture:
- Cover the mixture and refrigerate for at least 2 hours or until thoroughly chilled.

Churn in Ice Cream Maker:
- Pour the chilled mango mixture into an ice cream maker and churn according to the manufacturer's instructions until it reaches a sorbet-like consistency.

Transfer to Container:
- Transfer the churned sorbet into a lidded container, spreading it evenly.

Freeze Until Firm:
- Freeze the sorbet for at least 4 hours or overnight to achieve a firmer texture.

Serve and Garnish:
- Scoop the mango sorbet into bowls or cones. Garnish with additional mango slices or a sprig of mint if desired.

Note:

- If you don't have an ice cream maker, you can pour the mixture into a shallow dish, freeze it, and use a fork to break up ice crystals every 30 minutes until it reaches the desired consistency.

Variations:

- Add a splash of coconut milk to the mixture for a tropical coconut mango sorbet.
- Experiment with other fruit combinations, such as pineapple or passion fruit, for unique sorbet flavors.

Enjoy the refreshing and tropical goodness of homemade Mango Sorbet on a hot summer day!

Peach Cobbler

Ingredients:

For the Peach Filling:

- 6 cups fresh or canned peaches, peeled and sliced
- 1 cup granulated sugar
- 1 tablespoon lemon juice
- 1 teaspoon vanilla extract
- 2 tablespoons cornstarch

For the Cobbler Topping:

- 1 cup all-purpose flour
- 1 cup granulated sugar
- 1 teaspoon baking powder
- 1/2 teaspoon salt
- 1/2 cup unsalted butter, melted
- 1/2 cup milk
- 1 teaspoon vanilla extract

For Garnish:

- Powdered sugar (optional)
- Vanilla ice cream or whipped cream (optional)

Instructions:

Preheat the Oven:
- Preheat your oven to 375°F (190°C).

Prepare Peach Filling:
- In a large mixing bowl, combine sliced peaches, granulated sugar, lemon juice, vanilla extract, and cornstarch. Mix well until the peaches are evenly coated. Set aside.

Make Cobbler Topping:

- In another bowl, whisk together flour, sugar, baking powder, and salt. Add melted butter, milk, and vanilla extract. Stir until just combined.

Assemble the Cobbler:
- Pour the peach filling into a greased 9x13-inch baking dish. Spoon dollops of the cobbler topping over the peaches.

Bake:
- Bake in the preheated oven for 40-45 minutes or until the topping is golden brown, and the peach filling is bubbly.

Cool Slightly:
- Allow the peach cobbler to cool for about 15 minutes before serving.

Serve:
- Serve the peach cobbler warm. Dust with powdered sugar if desired and top with vanilla ice cream or whipped cream for an extra treat.

Variations:

- Add a pinch of cinnamon or nutmeg to the peach filling for a hint of spice.
- Mix chopped nuts (such as pecans or almonds) into the cobbler topping for added crunch.

This classic Peach Cobbler recipe is a delightful way to enjoy the sweet, juicy flavors of fresh peaches with a warm and comforting cobbler topping. Perfect for family gatherings or a cozy dessert any time of the year!

Strawberry Shortcake

Ingredients:

For the Shortcakes:

    2 cups all-purpose flour
    1/4 cup granulated sugar
    1 tablespoon baking powder
    1/2 teaspoon salt
    1/2 cup unsalted butter, cold and cut into small pieces
    2/3 cup milk
    1 teaspoon vanilla extract

For the Strawberries:

    4 cups fresh strawberries, hulled and sliced
    1/4 cup granulated sugar

For the Whipped Cream:

    1 cup heavy cream
    2 tablespoons powdered sugar
    1 teaspoon vanilla extract

Instructions:

Preheat the Oven:
- Preheat your oven to 425°F (220°C).

Prepare Shortcakes:
- In a large bowl, whisk together the flour, sugar, baking powder, and salt. Add the cold butter pieces and use a pastry cutter or your fingers to cut the butter into the dry ingredients until the mixture resembles coarse crumbs.

Combine Wet Ingredients:
- In a separate bowl, mix the milk and vanilla extract. Pour this mixture into the flour-butter mixture and stir until just combined.

Form Shortcakes:

- Turn the dough out onto a floured surface and gently knead it a few times. Pat the dough to about 3/4-inch thickness. Use a round biscuit cutter to cut out shortcakes and place them on a baking sheet.

Bake:
- Bake in the preheated oven for 12-15 minutes or until the shortcakes are golden brown. Allow them to cool on a wire rack.

Prepare Strawberries:
- In a bowl, combine sliced strawberries with sugar. Let them sit for about 15 minutes to release their juices and create a natural syrup.

Make Whipped Cream:
- In a chilled bowl, whip the heavy cream, powdered sugar, and vanilla extract until stiff peaks form.

Assemble Strawberry Shortcakes:
- Slice the shortcakes in half horizontally. Spoon a generous amount of strawberries onto the bottom half, add a dollop of whipped cream, and top with the other half of the shortcake.

Serve:
- Serve immediately and enjoy this classic Strawberry Shortcake!

Variations:

- Add a splash of balsamic vinegar to the strawberries for a tangy twist.
- Mix in other berries like blueberries or raspberries for a mixed berry shortcake.

This Strawberry Shortcake recipe brings together the perfect combination of tender shortcakes, sweet strawberries, and fluffy whipped cream for a delightful and iconic dessert.

Lemon Blueberry Cheesecake Bars

Ingredients:

For the Crust:

    2 cups graham cracker crumbs
    1/2 cup unsalted butter, melted
    1/4 cup granulated sugar

For the Cheesecake Filling:

    3 packages (24 ounces) cream cheese, softened
    1 cup granulated sugar
    3 large eggs
    1/4 cup sour cream
    1/4 cup all-purpose flour
    Zest of 1 lemon
    1 tablespoon lemon juice
    1 teaspoon vanilla extract

For the Blueberry Swirl:

    1 cup fresh or frozen blueberries
    2 tablespoons granulated sugar
    1 tablespoon water
    1 tablespoon lemon juice

Instructions:

Preheat the Oven:
- Preheat your oven to 325°F (163°C). Line a 9x13-inch baking pan with parchment paper, leaving an overhang for easy removal.

Prepare the Crust:
- In a bowl, combine graham cracker crumbs, melted butter, and sugar. Press the mixture firmly into the bottom of the prepared pan to create an even crust.

Bake the Crust:
- Bake the crust in the preheated oven for 10 minutes. Remove and let it cool while preparing the filling.

Make the Blueberry Swirl:
- In a small saucepan, combine blueberries, sugar, water, and lemon juice. Simmer over medium heat, stirring occasionally, until the blueberries break down and the mixture thickens. Remove from heat and let it cool.

Prepare Cheesecake Filling:
- In a large bowl, beat the cream cheese and sugar until smooth and creamy. Add eggs one at a time, beating well after each addition. Mix in sour cream, flour, lemon zest, lemon juice, and vanilla extract until well combined.

Assemble and Swirl:
- Pour the cream cheese mixture over the cooled crust. Spoon dollops of the blueberry mixture on top. Use a knife or skewer to swirl the blueberry mixture into the cream cheese for a marbled effect.

Bake the Cheesecake Bars:
- Bake in the preheated oven for 40-45 minutes or until the center is set. The edges should be slightly golden.

Cool and Chill:
- Allow the cheesecake bars to cool in the pan at room temperature, then refrigerate for at least 4 hours or overnight to set.

Slice and Serve:
- Once chilled, use the parchment paper overhang to lift the cheesecake out of the pan. Cut into bars and serve chilled.

Variations:

- Substitute other berries like raspberries or blackberries for a different fruity twist.
- Add a sprinkle of crumbled lemon cookies on top for extra texture.

These Lemon Blueberry Cheesecake Bars offer a delightful combination of creamy cheesecake, zesty lemon, and sweet blueberry swirls, making them a perfect treat for any occasion.

Watermelon Mint Salad

Ingredients:

    4 cups seedless watermelon, diced
    1 cup cucumber, peeled and diced
    1/2 cup red onion, thinly sliced
    1/4 cup fresh mint leaves, chopped
    1/4 cup feta cheese, crumbled
    2 tablespoons extra-virgin olive oil
    1 tablespoon balsamic vinegar
    Salt and black pepper, to taste

Instructions:

Prepare the Watermelon:
- Remove the rind from the watermelon and dice it into bite-sized cubes. Place the diced watermelon in a large mixing bowl.

Add Cucumber:
- Peel and dice the cucumber. Add it to the bowl with the watermelon.

Include Red Onion:
- Thinly slice the red onion and add it to the bowl with the watermelon and cucumber.

Toss with Mint:
- Chop the fresh mint leaves and sprinkle them over the watermelon mixture. Toss the ingredients gently to combine.

Add Feta Cheese:
- Crumble feta cheese over the salad and gently toss again.

Prepare Dressing:
- In a small bowl, whisk together the extra-virgin olive oil and balsamic vinegar. Season with salt and black pepper to taste.

Drizzle Dressing:
- Drizzle the dressing over the watermelon salad and toss to coat evenly.

Chill (Optional):
- Refrigerate the salad for about 30 minutes to allow the flavors to meld and the salad to chill.

Serve:

- Serve the Watermelon Mint Salad in individual bowls or as a refreshing side dish for picnics, barbecues, or summer gatherings.

Variations:

- Add a squeeze of fresh lime or lemon juice for an extra burst of citrus flavor.
- Incorporate arugula or baby spinach for a more substantial salad.
- Toasted pine nuts or sliced almonds can be a crunchy addition for added texture.

This Watermelon Mint Salad is a light, hydrating, and flavorful dish that perfectly captures the essence of summer. Enjoy its refreshing taste on a hot day or as a vibrant side dish at your next gathering.

Coconut Lime Popsicles

Ingredients:

1 can (14 ounces) coconut milk
1/2 cup coconut cream
1/2 cup granulated sugar
Zest and juice of 3 limes
1 teaspoon vanilla extract
Shredded coconut for garnish (optional)

Instructions:

Prepare Coconut Lime Mixture:
- In a mixing bowl, combine coconut milk, coconut cream, granulated sugar, lime zest, lime juice, and vanilla extract. Whisk until the sugar is completely dissolved.

Taste and Adjust:
- Taste the mixture and adjust the sweetness or acidity by adding more sugar or lime juice as needed.

Fill Popsicle Molds:
- Pour the coconut lime mixture into popsicle molds, leaving a little space at the top for expansion.

Insert Sticks:
- Place the popsicle sticks into the molds. If your molds come with a lid, use it to keep the sticks in place. If not, you can cover the molds with aluminum foil and insert the sticks through the foil.

Freeze:
- Place the popsicle molds in the freezer and let them freeze for at least 4-6 hours, or until completely set.

Optional Garnish:
- If desired, before the popsicles are fully set, sprinkle shredded coconut on top of each popsicle. Press gently to make it stick.

Unmold and Serve:
- Once fully frozen, run the molds briefly under warm water to loosen the popsicles. Gently pull the popsicles out of the molds.

Enjoy:
- Serve the Coconut Lime Popsicles immediately and enjoy this refreshing tropical treat.

Variations:

- Add a pinch of salt to enhance the flavors.
- Mix in finely chopped mint for a coconut-lime-mint twist.
- Dip the finished popsicles in melted white or dark chocolate and let them harden for a decadent touch.

These Coconut Lime Popsicles are a perfect combination of creamy coconut and zesty lime, creating a delightful frozen treat that's ideal for cooling down on a hot day.

Grilled Pineapple with Honey Glaze

Ingredients:

    1 whole pineapple, peeled, cored, and sliced into rings or wedges
    1/4 cup honey
    2 tablespoons unsalted butter, melted
    1 teaspoon ground cinnamon
    Optional: Vanilla ice cream or whipped cream for serving

Instructions:

  Preheat the Grill:
- Preheat your grill to medium-high heat.

  Prepare Pineapple:
- Peel the pineapple, remove the core, and slice it into rings or wedges, depending on your preference.

  Create Honey Glaze:
- In a small bowl, mix together honey, melted butter, and ground cinnamon to create the glaze.

  Brush Pineapple with Glaze:
- Brush the pineapple slices with the honey glaze, making sure to coat each piece evenly on both sides.

  Grill the Pineapple:
- Place the glazed pineapple slices on the preheated grill. Grill for 2-3 minutes on each side or until grill marks appear, and the pineapple caramelizes slightly.

  Baste with Glaze:
- While grilling, continue to baste the pineapple with the honey glaze, using a brush or spoon, for extra flavor.

  Remove from Grill:
- Once the pineapple has a golden caramelized exterior, remove it from the grill.

  Serve:
- Arrange the grilled pineapple on a serving platter. Drizzle any remaining honey glaze over the top.

  Optional:
- Serve the grilled pineapple with a scoop of vanilla ice cream or a dollop of whipped cream for a delightful dessert.

Variations:

- Sprinkle a pinch of chili powder or cayenne pepper on the pineapple slices for a spicy kick.
- Garnish with fresh mint leaves or a squeeze of lime juice before serving.
- Top with a sprinkle of toasted coconut for added texture.

Grilled Pineapple with Honey Glaze is a simple yet impressive dessert or side dish that brings out the natural sweetness of pineapple while adding a smoky caramelized flavor. Perfect for summer barbecues or as a sweet ending to any meal!

Raspberry Lemonade Cupcakes

Ingredients:

For the Cupcakes:

    1 1/2 cups all-purpose flour
    1 1/2 teaspoons baking powder
    1/4 teaspoon salt
    1/2 cup unsalted butter, softened
    1 cup granulated sugar
    2 large eggs
    1 teaspoon vanilla extract
    1/2 cup buttermilk
    Zest of 2 lemons
    1/4 cup fresh lemon juice

For the Raspberry Frosting:

    1 cup fresh or frozen raspberries
    1 cup unsalted butter, softened
    4 cups powdered sugar
    1 teaspoon vanilla extract
    2 tablespoons raspberry jam or preserves (optional, for extra flavor)

For Garnish:

    Fresh raspberries
    Lemon slices

Instructions:

    Preheat the Oven:
- Preheat your oven to 350°F (175°C). Line a cupcake tin with paper liners.

    Prepare Cupcake Batter:
- In a medium bowl, whisk together the flour, baking powder, and salt.

    Cream Butter and Sugar:
- In a large bowl, cream together the softened butter and granulated sugar until light and fluffy.

    Add Eggs and Vanilla:

- Beat in the eggs one at a time, then add the vanilla extract and continue to mix until well combined.

Alternate Dry Ingredients and Buttermilk:
- Gradually add the dry ingredients to the wet ingredients, alternating with buttermilk. Begin and end with the dry ingredients.

Add Lemon Zest and Juice:
- Mix in the lemon zest and fresh lemon juice until the batter is smooth and well incorporated.

Fill Cupcake Liners:
- Spoon the batter into the cupcake liners, filling each about 2/3 full.

Bake:
- Bake in the preheated oven for 18-20 minutes or until a toothpick inserted into the center comes out clean. Allow the cupcakes to cool completely.

Prepare Raspberry Frosting:
- In a blender or food processor, puree the raspberries until smooth. Strain the puree to remove seeds, if desired.

Make Raspberry Buttercream:
- In a large bowl, beat the softened butter until creamy. Gradually add the powdered sugar, vanilla extract, and raspberry puree. If you want a more intense raspberry flavor, add raspberry jam or preserves.

Frost Cupcakes:
- Once the cupcakes are completely cooled, frost them with the raspberry buttercream using a piping bag or spatula.

Garnish:
- Garnish each cupcake with a fresh raspberry and a slice of lemon.

Serve:
- Serve and enjoy these delightful Raspberry Lemonade Cupcakes!

Variations:

- Fill the cupcakes with a small dollop of raspberry jam for a surprise burst of flavor.
- Top with a sprinkle of lemon zest for extra citrus freshness.
- Experiment with different berry combinations in the frosting, such as a mix of raspberries and strawberries.

These Raspberry Lemonade Cupcakes are a burst of summer flavors, combining the zing of lemons with the sweetness of raspberries. They're perfect for celebrations, parties, or any time you want a delightful treat!

Key Lime Pie

Ingredients:

For the Graham Cracker Crust:

- 1 1/2 cups graham cracker crumbs
- 1/3 cup granulated sugar
- 1/2 cup unsalted butter, melted

For the Key Lime Filling:

- 4 large egg yolks
- 1 can (14 ounces) sweetened condensed milk
- 1/2 cup key lime juice (freshly squeezed if possible)
- Zest of 2 limes (for extra flavor, optional)

For the Whipped Cream Topping:

- 1 cup heavy cream
- 2 tablespoons powdered sugar
- 1/2 teaspoon vanilla extract

Instructions:

Preheat the Oven:
- Preheat your oven to 350°F (175°C).

Prepare Graham Cracker Crust:
- In a bowl, mix the graham cracker crumbs, granulated sugar, and melted butter until well combined. Press the mixture into the bottom and up the sides of a 9-inch pie dish to form the crust.

Bake the Crust:
- Bake the crust in the preheated oven for 8-10 minutes or until it is set. Remove from the oven and allow it to cool while you prepare the filling.

Make Key Lime Filling:

- In a large bowl, beat the egg yolks until they are pale and slightly thickened. Add the sweetened condensed milk, key lime juice, and lime zest (if using). Mix until well combined.

Pour into Crust:
- Pour the key lime filling into the prepared graham cracker crust, spreading it evenly.

Bake the Pie:
- Bake the pie in the oven for 15-18 minutes or until the center is set. It should still have a slight jiggle when gently shaken.

Cool and Chill:
- Allow the key lime pie to cool at room temperature, then refrigerate for at least 4 hours or overnight to set.

Prepare Whipped Cream Topping:
- In a chilled bowl, whip the heavy cream, powdered sugar, and vanilla extract until stiff peaks form.

Top the Pie:
- Once the key lime pie is fully chilled, spread or pipe the whipped cream on top.

Serve:
- Slice and serve the Key Lime Pie chilled. Optionally, garnish with additional lime zest or thin lime slices.

Variations:

- Use regular limes if key limes are not available, though the flavor will be slightly different.
- Toast shredded coconut and sprinkle it on top of the whipped cream for added texture.
- Drizzle the pie slices with a raspberry or mango coulis for a fruity twist.

This Key Lime Pie recipe delivers a perfect balance of sweetness and tartness, making it a classic and refreshing dessert, especially during warm weather.

Blackberry Lemon Sorbet

Ingredients:

3 cups fresh blackberries
3/4 cup granulated sugar
1 cup water
Zest of 2 lemons
1/2 cup fresh lemon juice (approximately 4 lemons)

Instructions:

Prepare Simple Syrup:
- In a small saucepan, combine sugar and water over medium heat. Stir until the sugar dissolves completely. Allow it to cool to room temperature.

Puree Blackberries:
- In a blender or food processor, puree the fresh blackberries until smooth.

Strain Blackberry Puree:
- Pass the blackberry puree through a fine-mesh sieve or cheesecloth to remove seeds and obtain a smooth liquid.

Combine Ingredients:
- In a mixing bowl, combine the blackberry puree, simple syrup, lemon zest, and fresh lemon juice. Mix well to ensure all ingredients are well combined.

Chill Mixture:
- Refrigerate the mixture for at least 2 hours or until thoroughly chilled.

Churn in Ice Cream Maker:
- Pour the chilled blackberry lemon mixture into an ice cream maker and churn according to the manufacturer's instructions until it reaches a sorbet-like consistency.

Transfer to Container:
- Transfer the churned sorbet into a lidded container, spreading it evenly.

Freeze Until Firm:
- Freeze the sorbet for at least 4 hours or overnight to achieve a firmer texture.

Serve:
- Scoop the Blackberry Lemon Sorbet into bowls or cones. Garnish with fresh blackberries or a twist of lemon if desired.

Variations:

- For a hint of freshness, add a handful of finely chopped mint leaves to the blackberry puree before churning.
- Experiment with other berries, such as raspberries or blueberries, to create a mixed berry sorbet.

This Blackberry Lemon Sorbet is a delightful and refreshing frozen treat, combining the bold sweetness of blackberries with the citrusy brightness of lemons. Enjoy its vibrant flavor on a hot day or as a palate cleanser between courses.

Orange Creamsicle Smoothie

Ingredients:

1 cup fresh orange juice (about 3-4 oranges)
1/2 cup plain Greek yogurt
1 medium banana, frozen
1/2 cup vanilla-flavored almond milk (or any milk of your choice)
1 teaspoon vanilla extract
1 tablespoon honey or maple syrup (optional, depending on sweetness preference)
Ice cubes (optional, for a colder and thicker smoothie)

Instructions:

Prepare Ingredients:
- Squeeze fresh oranges to obtain 1 cup of orange juice. Peel and freeze the banana ahead of time.

Assemble in Blender:
- In a blender, combine the fresh orange juice, frozen banana, Greek yogurt, vanilla-flavored almond milk, vanilla extract, and honey (if using).

Blend Until Smooth:
- Blend the ingredients on high speed until the mixture is smooth and creamy. If you prefer a thicker consistency, you can add a handful of ice cubes and blend again.

Taste and Adjust:
- Taste the smoothie and adjust the sweetness by adding more honey or maple syrup if needed.

Serve:
- Pour the Orange Creamsicle Smoothie into glasses and serve immediately.

Variations:

- Add a tablespoon of chia seeds or flaxseeds for an extra nutritional boost.
- Incorporate a scoop of vanilla protein powder for added protein.
- Garnish with orange slices or a sprinkle of grated orange zest for a decorative touch.

This Orange Creamsicle Smoothie is a delicious and refreshing way to enjoy the classic combination of citrusy oranges and creamy vanilla. It's perfect for a quick and nutritious breakfast or a delightful afternoon pick-me-up.

Mixed Berry Crisp

Ingredients:

For the Berry Filling:

    4 cups mixed berries (strawberries, blueberries, raspberries, blackberries)
    1/2 cup granulated sugar
    2 tablespoons cornstarch
    1 tablespoon lemon juice
    Zest of 1 lemon

For the Crisp Topping:

    1 cup old-fashioned rolled oats
    1/2 cup all-purpose flour
    1/2 cup packed brown sugar
    1/4 teaspoon salt
    1/2 cup unsalted butter, cold and cut into small pieces

Optional Garnish:

- Vanilla ice cream or whipped cream for serving

Instructions:

    Preheat the Oven:
- Preheat your oven to 350°F (175°C).

    Prepare the Berry Filling:
- In a large bowl, combine the mixed berries, granulated sugar, cornstarch, lemon juice, and lemon zest. Toss until the berries are well coated.

    Transfer to Baking Dish:
- Transfer the mixed berries to a greased 9x9-inch (or similar size) baking dish, spreading them out evenly.

    Prepare the Crisp Topping:
- In a separate bowl, mix together the rolled oats, all-purpose flour, brown sugar, and salt. Add the cold, diced butter pieces. Use your fingers or a pastry cutter to incorporate the butter into the dry ingredients until the mixture resembles coarse crumbs.

    Top the Berries:

- Sprinkle the crisp topping evenly over the mixed berries in the baking dish.

Bake:
- Bake in the preheated oven for 35-40 minutes or until the berry filling is bubbly, and the crisp topping is golden brown.

Cool Slightly:
- Allow the mixed berry crisp to cool for 10-15 minutes before serving.

Serve:
- Serve the mixed berry crisp warm, either on its own or topped with a scoop of vanilla ice cream or a dollop of whipped cream.

Variations:

- Add a handful of chopped nuts (such as almonds or pecans) to the crisp topping for extra crunch.
- Experiment with different combinations of berries, such as blackberries, raspberries, and blueberries, to suit your taste.

This Mixed Berry Crisp is a delightful dessert that showcases the natural sweetness of mixed berries, topped with a crunchy and flavorful oat topping. It's a perfect treat for any season and can be enjoyed on its own or with a scoop of your favorite ice cream.

Kiwi Strawberry Popsicles

Ingredients:

2 cups fresh strawberries, hulled and halved
3 ripe kiwi, peeled and sliced
1/4 cup honey or maple syrup (adjust according to sweetness preference)
1 cup water
1 tablespoon fresh lime or lemon juice

Instructions:

Prepare the Fruit:
- Wash and prepare the strawberries by hulling and halving them. Peel and slice the ripe kiwi.

Make Strawberry Puree:
- In a blender, puree the strawberries until smooth. If needed, add a little water to help with blending.

Make Kiwi Puree:
- In a separate blender or rinse the strawberry blender, puree the kiwi until smooth. Again, add water if necessary.

Sweeten the Purees:
- In each fruit puree (strawberry and kiwi), mix in honey or maple syrup to sweeten. Adjust the sweetness according to your taste.

Prepare Popsicle Mixture:
- Fill each popsicle mold by alternating layers of strawberry puree and kiwi puree. You can use a spoon or pour the puree carefully to create distinct layers.

Create Swirls:
- Use a skewer or popsicle stick to gently swirl the layers for a marbled effect.

Mix Lime or Lemon Juice:
- In a small bowl, mix the lime or lemon juice with water. Pour a little of this mixture over each layer to help set the popsicles and add a citrusy kick.

Insert Popsicle Sticks:
- Insert popsicle sticks into the molds, making sure they stand upright.

Freeze:

- Place the popsicle molds in the freezer and let them freeze for at least 4-6 hours or until fully set.

Unmold and Serve:
- Once the Kiwi Strawberry Popsicles are fully frozen, run the molds briefly under warm water to loosen the popsicles. Gently pull them out of the molds.

Enjoy:
- Serve and enjoy these refreshing homemade Kiwi Strawberry Popsicles!

Variations:

- Add small pieces of diced kiwi or strawberry chunks to each layer for added texture.
- Mix in a handful of fresh mint leaves to one of the purees for a hint of herbal freshness.
- Experiment with different berries like raspberries or blueberries for a mixed berry popsicle.

These Kiwi Strawberry Popsicles offer a delightful combination of sweet strawberries and tangy kiwi, making them a perfect treat for cooling down on a hot day or satisfying your sweet cravings in a healthy way.

Pineapple Upside-Down Cake

Ingredients:

For the Pineapple Topping:

    1/2 cup unsalted butter
    1 cup packed brown sugar
    1 can (20 ounces) pineapple slices (or fresh pineapple rings)
    Maraschino cherries, for garnish

For the Cake Batter:

    1 1/2 cups all-purpose flour
    1 1/2 teaspoons baking powder
    1/4 teaspoon salt
    1/2 cup unsalted butter, softened
    1 cup granulated sugar
    2 large eggs
    1 teaspoon vanilla extract
    1/2 cup pineapple juice (from the can or fresh)

Instructions:

Preheat the Oven:
- Preheat your oven to 350°F (175°C).

Prepare Pineapple Topping:
- In a saucepan, melt 1/2 cup of butter over low heat. Add the brown sugar and stir until well combined and melted. Pour this mixture into the bottom of a greased 9-inch round cake pan.

Arrange Pineapple Slices:
- Arrange the pineapple slices over the brown sugar mixture in the cake pan. Place a maraschino cherry in the center of each pineapple slice.

Prepare Cake Batter:
- In a bowl, whisk together the flour, baking powder, and salt.

Cream Butter and Sugar:

- In a separate large bowl, cream together 1/2 cup softened butter and granulated sugar until light and fluffy.

Add Eggs and Vanilla:
- Add the eggs one at a time, beating well after each addition. Mix in the vanilla extract.

Combine Dry Ingredients:
- Gradually add the dry ingredients to the butter and sugar mixture, alternating with the pineapple juice. Begin and end with the dry ingredients, mixing until just combined.

Pour Batter Over Pineapple:
- Pour the cake batter evenly over the arranged pineapple slices in the cake pan.

Bake:
- Bake in the preheated oven for 40-45 minutes or until a toothpick inserted into the center comes out clean.

Cooling and Inverting:
- Allow the cake to cool in the pan for 10-15 minutes. Run a knife around the edges to loosen the cake, then invert it onto a serving plate.

Serve:
- Serve the Pineapple Upside-Down Cake warm. Slice and enjoy!

Variations:

- Add a pinch of cinnamon or nutmeg to the dry ingredients for a warm, spiced flavor.
- Include a handful of shredded coconut to the pineapple topping for extra texture.
- Serve with a dollop of whipped cream or a scoop of vanilla ice cream for a delightful dessert.

This classic Pineapple Upside-Down Cake is a timeless and delicious dessert that showcases the sweetness of caramelized pineapple and the moist, flavorful cake beneath. Perfect for any occasion!

Blueberry Lemon Scones

Ingredients:

For the Scones:

    2 cups all-purpose flour
    1/3 cup granulated sugar
    1 tablespoon baking powder
    1/2 teaspoon salt
    Zest of 1 lemon
    1/2 cup unsalted butter, cold and cut into small pieces
    1 cup fresh or frozen blueberries
    2/3 cup whole milk or heavy cream
    1 teaspoon vanilla extract

For the Lemon Glaze:

    1 cup powdered sugar
    2 tablespoons fresh lemon juice
    Zest of 1 lemon

Instructions:

Preheat the Oven:
- Preheat your oven to 400°F (200°C). Line a baking sheet with parchment paper.

Prepare the Scones:
- In a large bowl, whisk together the flour, sugar, baking powder, salt, and lemon zest.

Cut in Butter:
- Add the cold, diced butter to the dry ingredients. Use a pastry cutter or your fingers to cut the butter into the flour mixture until it resembles coarse crumbs.

Add Blueberries:
- Gently fold in the blueberries, making sure they are evenly distributed in the mixture.

Combine Wet Ingredients:
- In a separate bowl, mix together the milk (or heavy cream) and vanilla extract.

Form Dough:
- Pour the wet ingredients into the flour-butter mixture. Stir until just combined. Be careful not to overmix.

Shape and Cut Scones:
- Turn the dough out onto a floured surface and knead it a few times. Pat the dough into a circle about 1 inch thick. Use a round cutter to cut out scones and place them on the prepared baking sheet.

Bake:
- Bake in the preheated oven for 15-18 minutes or until the scones are golden brown on top.

Make Lemon Glaze:
- While the scones are baking, prepare the lemon glaze. In a bowl, whisk together the powdered sugar, fresh lemon juice, and lemon zest until smooth.

Glaze the Scones:
- Once the scones are out of the oven and slightly cooled, drizzle the lemon glaze over the top of each scone.

Serve:
- Allow the glaze to set for a few minutes, then serve the Blueberry Lemon Scones warm or at room temperature.

Variations:

- Add a handful of chopped nuts, such as almonds or pecans, to the dough for extra crunch.
- Replace the lemon glaze with a simple vanilla glaze for a slightly different flavor.
- Mix in a tablespoon of poppy seeds to the dough for a Blueberry Lemon Poppy Seed variation.

These Blueberry Lemon Scones are a delightful combination of tender, flaky scones bursting with juicy blueberries and topped with a zesty lemon glaze. Enjoy them with a cup of tea or coffee for a perfect breakfast or afternoon treat.

Mint Chocolate Chip Ice Cream

Ingredients:

For the Ice Cream Base:

    2 cups heavy cream
    1 cup whole milk
    3/4 cup granulated sugar
    1 teaspoon pure vanilla extract

For the Mint Flavor:

    2 cups fresh mint leaves, packed
    1/2 cup granulated sugar

For the Chocolate Chips:

    1 cup dark chocolate, chopped or chocolate chips

Instructions:

Prepare Mint Infusion:
- In a saucepan, combine the fresh mint leaves and 1/2 cup sugar. Heat over medium heat until the sugar dissolves, and the mint leaves release their flavor. Remove from heat and let it cool.

Strain Mint Mixture:
- Strain the mint mixture to remove the leaves, pressing them to extract as much flavor as possible. Set aside the mint-infused sugar syrup.

Make Ice Cream Base:
- In a mixing bowl, whisk together heavy cream, whole milk, vanilla extract, and the mint-infused sugar syrup. Mix until the sugar is completely dissolved.

Chill Mixture:
- Cover the mixture and refrigerate for at least 4 hours or overnight to allow the flavors to meld and the mixture to chill.

Churn Ice Cream:

- Pour the chilled mixture into an ice cream maker and churn according to the manufacturer's instructions until it reaches a soft-serve consistency.

Add Chocolate Chips:
- During the last few minutes of churning, add the chopped chocolate or chocolate chips.

Transfer to Container:
- Transfer the mint chocolate chip ice cream to a lidded container, spreading it evenly.

Freeze Until Firm:
- Freeze the ice cream for at least 4 hours or overnight to achieve a firmer texture.

Serve:
- Scoop the Mint Chocolate Chip Ice Cream into bowls or cones. Enjoy!

Variations:

- For an extra green color, you can add a few drops of green food coloring to the ice cream base.
- Experiment with different types of chocolate, such as milk chocolate or white chocolate.
- Crush mint cookies and fold them into the ice cream for a mint chocolate cookie variation.

This Mint Chocolate Chip Ice Cream is a delightful blend of refreshing mint and rich chocolate. It's perfect for cooling down on a hot day or satisfying your sweet tooth with a classic and beloved flavor combination.

Cherry Almond Galette

Ingredients:

For the Galette Dough:

- 1 1/4 cups all-purpose flour
- 1/4 cup almond flour (ground almonds)
- 1 tablespoon granulated sugar
- 1/2 teaspoon salt
- 1/2 cup unsalted butter, cold and cut into small cubes
- 3-4 tablespoons ice water

For the Cherry Filling:

- 3 cups fresh cherries, pitted and halved
- 1/2 cup granulated sugar
- 2 tablespoons cornstarch
- 1 tablespoon lemon juice
- 1/2 teaspoon almond extract

For Assembly:

- 2 tablespoons almond meal (for sprinkling)
- 1 tablespoon sliced almonds (for garnish)
- 1 tablespoon turbinado sugar (for sprinkling)
- Egg wash (1 beaten egg with a splash of water)

Instructions:

Prepare Galette Dough:
- In a food processor, combine all-purpose flour, almond flour, granulated sugar, and salt. Add cold butter cubes and pulse until the mixture resembles coarse crumbs. Slowly add ice water, one tablespoon at a time, and pulse until the dough comes together.

Form Dough:
- Turn the dough out onto a floured surface, gather it into a ball, and flatten it into a disk. Wrap in plastic wrap and refrigerate for at least 30 minutes.

Preheat Oven:
- Preheat your oven to 375°F (190°C).

Prepare Cherry Filling:
- In a bowl, combine halved cherries, granulated sugar, cornstarch, lemon juice, and almond extract. Toss until the cherries are evenly coated. Let the mixture sit for a few minutes to allow the flavors to meld.

Roll Out Dough:
- On a floured surface, roll out the chilled galette dough into a rough circle about 12 inches in diameter.

Assemble Galette:
- Transfer the rolled-out dough onto a parchment-lined baking sheet. Sprinkle the center of the dough with almond meal, leaving a border around the edges. Arrange the cherry filling over the almond meal.

Fold Edges:
- Gently fold the edges of the dough over the cherries, creating a rustic border. Press the edges slightly to seal.

Brush with Egg Wash:
- Brush the folded edges of the galette with the egg wash. This gives the galette a golden-brown finish when baked.

Sprinkle with Sliced Almonds and Turbinado Sugar:
- Sprinkle sliced almonds over the cherries. Dust the entire galette, including the edges, with turbinado sugar for a sweet crunch.

Bake:
- Bake in the preheated oven for 35-40 minutes or until the crust is golden and the cherry filling is bubbly.

Cool and Serve:
- Allow the Cherry Almond Galette to cool on the baking sheet for a few minutes before transferring it to a wire rack. Serve warm or at room temperature.

Variations:

- Add a handful of fresh raspberries or blueberries to the cherry filling for a mixed berry galette.
- Drizzle a simple glaze made with powdered sugar and milk over the galette after it has cooled for an extra touch of sweetness.

This Cherry Almond Galette is a simple and elegant dessert that captures the sweet and tart flavors of fresh cherries, enhanced by the nutty richness of almond. Enjoy it with a scoop of vanilla ice cream for a delightful treat.

Honeydew Basil Sorbet

Ingredients:

4 cups honeydew melon, peeled, seeded, and cubed
1/2 cup granulated sugar
1/2 cup water
1/4 cup fresh basil leaves, chopped
2 tablespoons fresh lime juice

Instructions:

Prepare Honeydew:
- Peel, seed, and cube the honeydew melon to get approximately 4 cups.

Make Simple Syrup:
- In a saucepan, combine sugar and water over medium heat. Stir until the sugar completely dissolves, creating a simple syrup. Remove from heat and let it cool.

Infuse with Basil:
- Add chopped basil leaves to the simple syrup while it's still warm. Let the basil infuse into the syrup as it cools.

Blend Honeydew:
- In a blender, puree the honeydew cubes until smooth.

Strain and Combine:
- Strain the basil-infused simple syrup to remove the basil leaves. Combine the honeydew puree, strained simple syrup, and fresh lime juice in a bowl. Mix well.

Chill Mixture:
- Refrigerate the mixture for at least 2 hours or until thoroughly chilled.

Churn in Ice Cream Maker:
- Pour the chilled honeydew basil mixture into an ice cream maker and churn according to the manufacturer's instructions until it reaches a sorbet-like consistency.

Transfer to Container:
- Transfer the churned sorbet into a lidded container, spreading it evenly.

Freeze Until Firm:
- Freeze the sorbet for at least 4 hours or overnight to achieve a firm texture.

Serve:
- Scoop the Honeydew Basil Sorbet into bowls or cones. Garnish with fresh basil leaves for an extra touch.

Variations:

- For added texture, fold in finely chopped fresh basil into the sorbet before freezing.
- Replace lime juice with lemon juice for a slightly different citrus flavor.
- Create a refreshing dessert by serving the sorbet in hollowed-out honeydew halves.

This Honeydew Basil Sorbet is a unique and refreshing frozen treat that combines the subtle sweetness of honeydew with the aromatic essence of fresh basil. It's a perfect way to cool down on a hot day or to cleanse the palate after a meal.

Peach Melba

Ingredients:

For the Poached Peaches:

- 4 ripe peaches, peeled, pitted, and halved
- 1 cup water
- 1/2 cup granulated sugar
- 1 vanilla bean, split (or 1 teaspoon vanilla extract)

For the Raspberry Sauce:

- 1 1/2 cups fresh raspberries (or frozen, thawed)
- 1/4 cup granulated sugar
- 1 tablespoon lemon juice

For Serving:

- Vanilla ice cream
- Sliced almonds (optional, for garnish)
- Fresh mint leaves (optional, for garnish)

Instructions:

Poach the Peaches:
- In a saucepan, combine water and granulated sugar. Add the split vanilla bean (or vanilla extract). Bring the mixture to a simmer over medium heat.
- Gently place the peach halves into the simmering syrup. Poach for about 5-7 minutes or until the peaches are tender but not mushy.
- Using a slotted spoon, remove the poached peaches from the syrup and let them cool. Discard the vanilla bean.

Prepare Raspberry Sauce:
- In a blender or food processor, puree the raspberries until smooth. Strain the puree to remove the seeds, if desired.
- In a saucepan, combine the raspberry puree, granulated sugar, and lemon juice. Heat over medium heat, stirring occasionally, until the sugar is

dissolved and the sauce has slightly thickened. Remove from heat and let it cool.

Assemble Peach Melba:
- Place a poached peach half on a serving plate or bowl.
- Top each peach half with a scoop of vanilla ice cream.

Drizzle with Raspberry Sauce:
- Spoon the raspberry sauce over the top of the vanilla ice cream and poached peaches.

Garnish:
- Optionally, garnish with sliced almonds and fresh mint leaves for added texture and freshness.

Serve:
- Serve the Peach Melba immediately, allowing the warm poached peaches to contrast with the cold vanilla ice cream and the vibrant raspberry sauce.

Variations:

- Substitute other stone fruits like nectarines or apricots for the peaches.
- Experiment with different berry sauces, such as blackberry or mixed berry, for a unique twist.
- Add a drizzle of chocolate sauce or a sprinkle of grated chocolate for a decadent touch.

Peach Melba is a classic and elegant dessert that celebrates the natural sweetness of peaches, the tartness of raspberries, and the creamy richness of vanilla ice cream. It's a delightful treat that's perfect for summer or any special occasion.

Raspberry Swirl Cheesecake

Ingredients:

For the Crust:

- 2 cups graham cracker crumbs
- 1/2 cup unsalted butter, melted
- 1/4 cup granulated sugar

For the Cheesecake Filling:

- 4 packages (32 ounces total) cream cheese, softened
- 1 1/4 cups granulated sugar
- 1 teaspoon vanilla extract
- 4 large eggs
- 1 cup sour cream

For the Raspberry Swirl:

- 1 1/2 cups fresh or frozen raspberries
- 1/4 cup granulated sugar
- 2 tablespoons water
- 1 tablespoon lemon juice

Instructions:

Preheat the Oven:
- Preheat your oven to 325°F (163°C). Grease a 9-inch springform pan with butter or cooking spray.

Prepare the Crust:
- In a bowl, mix together graham cracker crumbs, melted butter, and sugar until well combined. Press the mixture into the bottom of the prepared springform pan to create an even crust.

Bake the Crust:
- Bake the crust in the preheated oven for 10 minutes. Remove from the oven and let it cool while preparing the cheesecake filling.

Prepare Raspberry Swirl:
- In a saucepan, combine raspberries, sugar, water, and lemon juice. Cook over medium heat, stirring occasionally, until the raspberries break down and the mixture thickens into a sauce. Remove from heat and strain to remove seeds. Allow the raspberry sauce to cool.

Make the Cheesecake Filling:
- In a large mixing bowl, beat the softened cream cheese until smooth. Add sugar and vanilla extract, and continue beating until well combined.
- Add the eggs one at a time, mixing well after each addition. Stir in the sour cream until the batter is creamy and smooth.

Assemble the Cheesecake:
- Pour the cream cheese filling over the baked crust in the springform pan. Smooth the top with a spatula.

Add Raspberry Swirl:
- Drop spoonfuls of the raspberry sauce onto the cheesecake batter. Use a knife or toothpick to create swirls by gently dragging it through the raspberry sauce and cheesecake batter.

Bake the Cheesecake:
- Bake in the preheated oven for about 55-65 minutes or until the center is set and the edges are slightly golden. The center might still jiggle slightly but will firm up as it cools.

Cool and Chill:
- Allow the cheesecake to cool in the oven with the door ajar for about an hour, then refrigerate for at least 4 hours or overnight to set.

Serve:
- Once fully chilled and set, remove the sides of the springform pan. Slice and serve the Raspberry Swirl Cheesecake. Optionally, garnish with fresh raspberries.

Variations:

- Add a tablespoon of cornstarch to the raspberry sauce if you want a thicker swirl.
- Experiment with different berry swirls, such as blueberry or blackberry, for variety.
- Top with a dollop of whipped cream or a drizzle of white chocolate for an extra touch.

This Raspberry Swirl Cheesecake is a delicious combination of rich and creamy cheesecake with the vibrant and tart flavor of raspberry swirls. It's a stunning dessert that's sure to impress your family and friends.

Lemon Poppy Seed Muffins

Ingredients:

Dry Ingredients:

    2 cups all-purpose flour
    1/2 cup granulated sugar
    1/4 cup poppy seeds
    2 teaspoons baking powder
    1/2 teaspoon baking soda
    1/4 teaspoon salt

Wet Ingredients:

    3/4 cup unsalted butter, melted and cooled
    1 cup plain Greek yogurt
    2 large eggs
    Zest of 2 lemons
    1/4 cup fresh lemon juice
    1 teaspoon vanilla extract

Glaze (Optional):

    1 cup powdered sugar
    2 tablespoons fresh lemon juice
    Zest of 1 lemon

Instructions:

    Preheat the Oven:
- Preheat your oven to 375°F (190°C). Line a muffin tin with paper liners or grease with cooking spray.

    Prepare Dry Ingredients:
- In a large bowl, whisk together the flour, sugar, poppy seeds, baking powder, baking soda, and salt.

    Mix Wet Ingredients:

- In another bowl, whisk together the melted butter, Greek yogurt, eggs, lemon zest, lemon juice, and vanilla extract.

Combine Wet and Dry Ingredients:
- Pour the wet ingredients into the bowl with the dry ingredients. Gently fold the ingredients together until just combined. Be careful not to overmix; a few lumps are okay.

Fill Muffin Cups:
- Spoon the batter into the prepared muffin cups, filling each about two-thirds full.

Bake:
- Bake in the preheated oven for 18-20 minutes or until a toothpick inserted into the center comes out clean or with a few moist crumbs.

Cool:
- Allow the muffins to cool in the tin for 5 minutes, then transfer them to a wire rack to cool completely.

Prepare Glaze (Optional):
- If using the glaze, whisk together the powdered sugar, lemon juice, and lemon zest until smooth. Drizzle the glaze over the cooled muffins.

Serve:
- Once the glaze has set, serve the Lemon Poppy Seed Muffins. Enjoy!

Variations:

- Add a handful of blueberries or raspberries to the batter for a fruity twist.
- Substitute part of the all-purpose flour with whole wheat flour for added fiber.
- Sprinkle a mixture of sugar and additional poppy seeds on top of the muffins before baking for a crunchy topping.

These Lemon Poppy Seed Muffins are moist, flavorful, and have a delightful citrusy kick.

Whether enjoyed for breakfast, brunch, or as a snack, they are sure to brighten your day!

Chocolate-Dipped Strawberries

Ingredients:

    1 pound fresh strawberries, washed and dried
    8 ounces high-quality dark or semi-sweet chocolate, chopped
    4 ounces white chocolate, chopped (for drizzling, optional)
    Toppings for decoration (chopped nuts, shredded coconut, sprinkles, etc.)

Instructions:

Prepare Strawberries:
- Ensure that the strawberries are completely dry as any moisture can cause the chocolate to seize. Line a baking sheet with parchment paper.

Melt Dark Chocolate:
- Place the dark or semi-sweet chocolate in a heatproof bowl. Melt the chocolate using a double boiler or in short intervals in the microwave, stirring frequently to prevent burning. Remove from heat when fully melted.

Dip Strawberries:
- Hold each strawberry by the stem and dip it into the melted chocolate, ensuring that most of the strawberry is coated. Allow excess chocolate to drip off.

Place on Parchment Paper:
- Place the dipped strawberries on the parchment-lined baking sheet, leaving a small space between each one.

Melt White Chocolate (Optional):
- If you want to drizzle white chocolate over the dipped strawberries, melt the white chocolate in the same manner as the dark chocolate.

Drizzle White Chocolate (Optional):
- Using a fork or a piping bag, drizzle the melted white chocolate over the dipped strawberries. This adds a decorative touch.

Add Toppings:
- While the chocolate is still wet, sprinkle the dipped strawberries with your choice of toppings, such as chopped nuts, shredded coconut, or sprinkles.

Set the Chocolate:
- Allow the chocolate-dipped strawberries to set at room temperature. You can also refrigerate them for faster setting.

Serve:
- Once the chocolate is fully set, transfer the chocolate-dipped strawberries to a serving plate or platter. Serve and enjoy!

Tips:

- Choose ripe and firm strawberries for the best results.
- Use high-quality chocolate for a smoother and more delicious coating.
- Experiment with different toppings to create a variety of chocolate-dipped strawberry treats.

Chocolate-dipped strawberries are a classic and elegant treat that's perfect for special occasions, romantic gestures, or simply satisfying your sweet cravings. Enjoy these delightful treats on their own or as a charming addition to your dessert table.

Vanilla Bean Ice Cream

Ingredients:

    2 cups heavy cream
    1 cup whole milk
    3/4 cup granulated sugar
    1 vanilla bean pod (or 2 teaspoons pure vanilla extract)
    6 large egg yolks

Instructions:

Prepare Vanilla Bean:
- If using a vanilla bean, split it lengthwise with a knife and scrape out the seeds. Place the seeds and the pod in a saucepan with the cream and milk. If using vanilla extract, skip this step.

Heat Cream and Milk:
- Heat the cream, milk, and vanilla bean (if using) in a saucepan over medium heat until it just starts to simmer. Do not boil.

Whisk Sugar and Egg Yolks:
- While the cream mixture is heating, whisk together the sugar and egg yolks in a separate bowl until pale and slightly thickened.

Temper Egg Mixture:
- Gradually pour a small amount of the hot cream mixture into the egg mixture, whisking constantly. This process, called tempering, prevents the eggs from curdling.

Combine Mixtures:
- Pour the tempered egg mixture back into the saucepan with the remaining cream mixture, stirring constantly

Cook Custard:
- Cook the custard over medium heat, stirring continuously, until it thickens and coats the back of a spoon. Be careful not to let it boil.

Strain and Cool:
- Strain the custard through a fine-mesh sieve into a clean bowl to remove the vanilla bean pod and any possible cooked egg bits. If using vanilla extract, add it at this stage. Let the custard cool to room temperature.

Chill:

- Cover the bowl with plastic wrap, ensuring it touches the surface of the custard to prevent a skin from forming. Refrigerate for at least 4 hours or overnight.

Churn in Ice Cream Maker:
- Once thoroughly chilled, churn the custard in an ice cream maker according to the manufacturer's instructions until it reaches a soft-serve consistency.

Transfer to Container:
- Transfer the churned ice cream to a lidded container, spreading it evenly.

Freeze Until Firm:
- Freeze the vanilla bean ice cream for at least 4 hours or overnight to achieve a firm texture.

Serve:
- Scoop the Vanilla Bean Ice Cream into bowls or cones. Enjoy!

Note:

- If you don't have an ice cream maker, you can pour the chilled custard into a lidded container and freeze it, stirring every 30 minutes until it reaches the desired consistency.

Making Vanilla Bean Ice Cream at home allows you to enjoy a rich and creamy treat with the natural flavors of vanilla. Serve it on its own, with a slice of pie, or as a delightful addition to various desserts.

Caramelized Banana Split

Ingredients:

For Caramelized Bananas:

    3 ripe bananas, peeled and sliced
    2 tablespoons unsalted butter
    2 tablespoons brown sugar
    1/2 teaspoon ground cinnamon (optional)

For Assembly:

    Vanilla ice cream
    Chocolate ice cream
    Strawberry ice cream
    Chocolate sauce
    Strawberry sauce or fresh strawberries, sliced
    Chopped nuts (such as walnuts or almonds)
    Whipped cream
    Maraschino cherries

Instructions:

    Caramelize Bananas:
- In a skillet over medium heat, melt the butter. Add the sliced bananas, brown sugar, and ground cinnamon (if using). Cook the bananas for 2-3 minutes on each side until they are caramelized and golden. Remove from heat.

    Assemble Banana Split:
- In a long dessert dish or individual bowls, arrange the caramelized banana slices.

    Add Ice Cream Scoops:
- Place scoops of vanilla, chocolate, and strawberry ice cream between the banana slices.

    Drizzle with Sauces:

- Drizzle chocolate sauce over the chocolate ice cream and strawberry sauce or add fresh sliced strawberries over the strawberry ice cream.

Top with Nuts:
- Sprinkle chopped nuts (walnuts or almonds) over the ice cream.

Add Whipped Cream:
- Dollop whipped cream on top of each ice cream scoop.

Garnish with Cherries:
- Finish by placing maraschino cherries on top of the whipped cream.

Serve Immediately:
- Serve the Caramelized Banana Split immediately while the ice cream is still cold and the caramelized bananas are warm.

Variations:

- Nutty Delight: Roll the caramelized bananas in chopped nuts (such as peanuts or pecans) before assembling the banana split for an extra crunch.
- Tropical Twist: Add a scoop of coconut or pineapple ice cream and drizzle with coconut cream for a tropical flavor.
- Double Chocolate: Use chocolate-covered bananas or chocolate-flavored whipped cream for a double chocolate experience.
- Healthy Option: Replace regular ice cream with frozen yogurt or low-fat ice cream, and opt for a sugar-free caramelized banana option.

This Caramelized Banana Split is a delicious and indulgent dessert that combines the sweetness of caramelized bananas with a variety of ice cream flavors and toppings. It's a classic treat with a warm and gooey twist!

Pomegranate Granita

Ingredients:

- 2 cups pomegranate juice (freshly squeezed or store-bought)
- 1/2 cup granulated sugar
- 1/4 cup water
- 2 tablespoons fresh lemon juice
- Pomegranate seeds for garnish (optional)
- Fresh mint leaves for garnish (optional)

Instructions:

Prepare Simple Syrup:
- In a small saucepan, combine the granulated sugar and water. Heat over medium heat, stirring occasionally, until the sugar dissolves completely. Remove from heat and let the simple syrup cool.

Mix Pomegranate Juice and Lemon Juice:
- In a mixing bowl, combine the pomegranate juice and fresh lemon juice.

Add Simple Syrup:
- Pour the cooled simple syrup into the pomegranate and lemon juice mixture. Stir well to combine.

Transfer to a Dish:
- Pour the mixture into a shallow, wide dish (such as a baking dish). The larger the surface area, the quicker the granita will freeze.

Freeze and Scrape:
- Place the dish in the freezer. After about 1-2 hours, when the edges start to freeze, use a fork to scrape the ice crystals. Repeat this process every 30 minutes for the next 3-4 hours. This creates a light and fluffy granita texture.

Fluff with a Fork:
- After the last scraping, fluff the entire mixture with a fork to ensure a light and fluffy consistency.

Serve:
- Spoon the Pomegranate Granita into serving glasses. Garnish with fresh pomegranate seeds and mint leaves if desired.

Enjoy:

- Serve immediately and enjoy the refreshing and icy taste of homemade Pomegranate Granita!

Variations:

- Minty Twist: Add a handful of finely chopped fresh mint leaves to the pomegranate mixture before freezing for a mint-infused granita.
- Citrussy Blend: Enhance the flavor with a splash of orange juice or a hint of grated orange zest.
- Adult Version: For a grown-up version, you can add a splash of vodka or your favorite spirit to the pomegranate mixture before freezing.
- Berries Galore: Mix in some fresh berries like raspberries or blueberries for added color and flavor.

This Pomegranate Granita is a delightful and refreshing dessert that's perfect for hot summer days. Its icy texture and vibrant flavor make it a fantastic way to enjoy the sweet and tart taste of pomegranate.

Coconut Mango Rice Pudding

Ingredients:

For the Rice Pudding:

    1 cup Arborio rice
    1 can (13.5 oz) coconut milk
    3 cups whole milk
    1/2 cup granulated sugar
    1/4 teaspoon salt
    1 teaspoon vanilla extract

For the Mango Puree:

    2 ripe mangoes, peeled and diced
    2 tablespoons honey or maple syrup
    1 tablespoon fresh lime juice

For Garnish:

    Toasted coconut flakes
    Sliced fresh mango
    Mint leaves

Instructions:

Make Rice Pudding:

    Rinse Rice:
- Rinse the Arborio rice under cold water until the water runs clear.

    Cook Rice:
- In a medium-sized saucepan, combine the coconut milk, whole milk, sugar, and salt. Bring to a gentle simmer over medium heat, stirring occasionally. Add the rinsed Arborio rice.

    Simmer and Stir:
- Reduce the heat to low and simmer, stirring frequently to prevent sticking, until the rice is cooked and the mixture has thickened, approximately 25-30 minutes.

    Add Vanilla:

- Stir in the vanilla extract during the last few minutes of cooking.

Cool:
- Remove the rice pudding from the heat and let it cool slightly. It will continue to thicken as it cools.

Make Mango Puree:

Blend Mangoes:
- In a blender, combine diced mangoes, honey or maple syrup, and fresh lime juice. Blend until smooth.

Assemble Coconut Mango Rice Pudding:

Layer:
- In serving glasses or bowls, layer the rice pudding and mango puree.

Chill:
- Refrigerate for at least 2 hours to allow the flavors to meld and the dessert to chill.

Garnish:
- Before serving, garnish with toasted coconut flakes, sliced fresh mango, and mint leaves.

Serve:
- Serve the Coconut Mango Rice Pudding chilled. Enjoy the tropical flavors!

Variations:

- Coconut Garnish: Sprinkle additional toasted coconut flakes on top for extra coconut flavor and texture.
- Nutty Crunch: Add a handful of chopped nuts (such as toasted almonds or cashews) as a crunchy topping.
- Spice it Up: Stir in a pinch of ground cardamom or cinnamon into the rice pudding for a warm and aromatic touch.
- Dairy-Free Option: Use coconut milk instead of whole milk for the rice pudding to make it entirely dairy-free.

This Coconut Mango Rice Pudding is a luscious and exotic dessert that combines creamy coconut-infused rice pudding with the sweet and tropical flavor of mango puree. It's a delightful treat that brings a taste of the tropics to your table.

Blueberry Lemonade Slushie

Ingredients:

    2 cups fresh or frozen blueberries
    1/2 cup freshly squeezed lemon juice (about 3-4 lemons)
    1/3 cup granulated sugar (adjust to taste)
    2 cups ice cubes
    1 cup cold water
    Fresh mint leaves for garnish (optional)
    Lemon slices for garnish (optional)

Instructions:

    Prepare Blueberries:
- If using fresh blueberries, rinse them under cold water. If using frozen blueberries, allow them to thaw slightly.

    Blend Blueberries:
- In a blender, combine the blueberries, freshly squeezed lemon juice, granulated sugar, ice cubes, and cold water.

    Blend Until Smooth:
- Blend the ingredients until smooth and slushie-like in consistency. Adjust the sweetness by adding more sugar if needed.

    Taste and Adjust:
- Taste the slushie and adjust the sweetness or tartness by adding more sugar or lemon juice, according to your preference.

    Serve:
- Pour the Blueberry Lemonade Slushie into glasses.

    Garnish (Optional):
- Garnish with fresh mint leaves and lemon slices for a decorative touch.

    Enjoy Immediately:
- Serve the Blueberry Lemonade Slushie immediately while it's icy and refreshing.

Variations:

- Berry Blend: Mix in other berries like raspberries or strawberries for a mixed berry slushie.

- Coconut Twist: Add a splash of coconut water or coconut milk for a hint of tropical flavor.
- Adult Version: For an adult version, you can spike the slushie with a shot of vodka or your favorite spirit.
- Herbal Infusion: Blend in a few basil or mint leaves with the blueberries for an herby twist.

This Blueberry Lemonade Slushie is a vibrant and thirst-quenching drink, perfect for hot summer days or as a refreshing treat anytime you crave a burst of fruity flavor. Enjoy the cool and tangy sensation of this delightful slushie!

Grilled Peaches with Cinnamon Sugar

Ingredients:

    4 ripe peaches, halved and pitted
    2 tablespoons melted unsalted butter
    2 tablespoons brown sugar
    1 teaspoon ground cinnamon
    Vanilla ice cream or Greek yogurt for serving (optional)
    Honey or maple syrup for drizzling (optional)
    Fresh mint leaves for garnish (optional)

Instructions:

Preheat the Grill:
- Preheat your grill to medium-high heat.

Prepare Peaches:
- Cut the peaches in half and remove the pits.

Brush with Butter:
- In a small bowl, mix the melted butter. Brush the cut sides of the peaches with the melted butter.

Sprinkle with Cinnamon Sugar:
- In another bowl, combine the brown sugar and ground cinnamon. Sprinkle the cinnamon sugar mixture evenly over the cut sides of the peaches.

Grill Peaches:
- Place the peaches on the preheated grill, cut side down. Grill for about 3-4 minutes or until grill marks appear.

Flip and Grill:
- Carefully flip the peaches using tongs. Grill for an additional 2-3 minutes on the other side until they are tender but still firm.

Serve:
- Remove the grilled peaches from the grill and transfer them to a serving plate.

Optional Toppings:
- Serve the grilled peaches on their own or with a scoop of vanilla ice cream or a dollop of Greek yogurt. Drizzle with honey or maple syrup for added sweetness.

Garnish (Optional):

- Garnish with fresh mint leaves for a pop of color and extra freshness.

Enjoy:
- Serve the Grilled Peaches with Cinnamon Sugar immediately while they are warm. Enjoy the delightful combination of smoky grilled flavor and sweet cinnamon sugar!

Variations:

- Spiced Yogurt: Mix a pinch of cinnamon and a drizzle of honey into Greek yogurt for a spiced yogurt topping.
- Nutty Crunch: Sprinkle chopped nuts (such as almonds or pecans) over the grilled peaches for added texture.
- Boozy Twist: For an adult version, brush the peaches with a mixture of melted butter and a splash of bourbon before grilling.
- Coconut Delight: Top the grilled peaches with a scoop of coconut ice cream or a sprinkle of shredded coconut for a tropical twist.

Grilled Peaches with Cinnamon Sugar is a simple yet elegant dessert that showcases the natural sweetness of ripe peaches enhanced by the warmth of cinnamon. It's a delightful treat that's perfect for summer gatherings or a cozy evening by the grill.

Strawberry Rhubarb Pie

Ingredients:

For the Pie Filling:

    3 cups fresh rhubarb, diced into 1/2-inch pieces
    3 cups fresh strawberries, hulled and sliced
    1 cup granulated sugar
    1/2 cup light brown sugar, packed
    1/4 cup cornstarch
    1 teaspoon ground cinnamon
    1/4 teaspoon salt
    1 tablespoon lemon juice
    1 teaspoon vanilla extract

For the Pie Crust:

    2 1/2 cups all-purpose flour
    1 cup unsalted butter, cold and cubed
    1 teaspoon salt
    1 tablespoon granulated sugar
    1/2 cup ice water

For Egg Wash:

    1 egg
    1 tablespoon water

Instructions:

Prepare Pie Crust:

    Cut Butter into Flour Mixture:
- In a large bowl, combine the flour, salt, and sugar. Add the cold, cubed butter and use a pastry cutter or your fingers to cut the butter into the flour until it resembles coarse crumbs.

Add Ice Water:
- Gradually add ice water, a tablespoon at a time, and mix until the dough just comes together. Divide the dough into two equal portions, shape into discs, wrap in plastic wrap, and refrigerate for at least 1 hour.

Prepare Pie Filling:

Preheat Oven:
- Preheat your oven to 400°F (200°C).

Roll Out Pie Crust:
- On a floured surface, roll out one disc of the pie crust to fit a 9-inch pie dish. Place it in the pie dish and trim any excess crust, leaving a slight overhang.

Make Filling:
- In a large bowl, combine diced rhubarb, sliced strawberries, granulated sugar, brown sugar, cornstarch, ground cinnamon, salt, lemon juice, and vanilla extract. Mix until well combined.

Fill Pie Shell:
- Spoon the strawberry rhubarb filling into the prepared pie crust.

Roll Out and Arrange Second Crust:
- Roll out the second disc of pie crust and either cover the pie with a full crust or cut strips to create a lattice pattern. If using a full crust, cut slits for ventilation.

Seal Edges:
- Seal the edges of the crust by crimping with a fork or your fingers. If using a lattice crust, weave the strips over the filling.

Egg Wash:

Prepare Egg Wash:
- In a small bowl, beat the egg with water to create an egg wash.

Brush Crust:
- Brush the top crust with the egg wash for a golden finish.

Bake:

Bake:

- Place the pie on a baking sheet to catch any drips. Bake in the preheated oven for 20 minutes. Reduce the oven temperature to 350°F (175°C) and continue baking for an additional 40-50 minutes or until the filling is bubbly, and the crust is golden brown.

Cool:
- Allow the Strawberry Rhubarb Pie to cool completely before slicing. This helps the filling set.

Serve:
- Slice and serve the pie on its own or with a scoop of vanilla ice cream.

Variations:

- Citrus Zest: Add the zest of an orange or lemon to the filling for a citrusy twist.
- Ginger Infusion: Add a teaspoon of grated fresh ginger to the filling for a hint of warmth.
- Almond Crust: Replace a portion of the all-purpose flour in the crust with almond flour for a nutty flavor.
- Oat Streusel Topping: Sprinkle an oat streusel topping over the pie before baking for added texture.

This Strawberry Rhubarb Pie is a classic and delightful dessert that beautifully balances the sweetness of strawberries with the tartness of rhubarb. It's perfect for showcasing the vibrant flavors of spring and early summer.

Mint Chocolate Brownie Bites

Ingredients:

For the Brownie Base:

    1/2 cup unsalted butter, melted
    1 cup granulated sugar
    2 large eggs
    1 teaspoon vanilla extract
    1/3 cup unsweetened cocoa powder
    1/2 cup all-purpose flour
    1/4 teaspoon salt

For the Mint Layer:

    2 cups powdered sugar
    1/4 cup unsalted butter, softened
    2 tablespoons heavy cream
    1/2 teaspoon peppermint extract
    Green food coloring (optional)

For the Chocolate Ganache:

    1/2 cup semi-sweet chocolate chips
    1/4 cup heavy cream

Instructions:

1. Preheat the Oven:

- Preheat your oven to 350°F (175°C). Grease a mini muffin tin or line it with mini cupcake liners.

2. Make the Brownie Base:

a. Mix Wet Ingredients:

- In a mixing bowl, combine melted butter and granulated sugar. Mix until well combined.

b. Add Eggs and Vanilla:

- Add eggs and vanilla extract to the butter-sugar mixture. Mix until smooth.

c. Incorporate Dry Ingredients:

- Sift in cocoa powder, all-purpose flour, and salt. Mix until just combined.

d. Fill Mini Muffin Tin:

- Spoon the brownie batter into the mini muffin tin, filling each cup about halfway.

e. Bake:

- Bake in the preheated oven for about 10-12 minutes or until a toothpick inserted into the center comes out with moist crumbs. Be careful not to overbake.

3. Make the Mint Layer:

a. Prepare Mint Filling:

- In a separate bowl, beat together powdered sugar, softened butter, heavy cream, peppermint extract, and green food coloring (if using) until smooth and creamy.

b. Fill Brownie Cups:

- Once the brownie bites have cooled, use a piping bag or a small spoon to add a layer of mint filling on top of each brownie base.

4. Make the Chocolate Ganache:

a. Heat Chocolate and Cream:

- In a microwave-safe bowl, heat chocolate chips and heavy cream in 20-second intervals, stirring each time, until the chocolate is fully melted and the mixture is smooth.

b. Top with Chocolate Ganache:

- Spoon or drizzle the chocolate ganache over the mint layer in each brownie bite.

5. Chill and Serve:

- Place the mint chocolate brownie bites in the refrigerator for at least 1 hour to allow the mint layer to set.
- Once set, remove from the refrigerator and serve. Optionally, garnish with additional mint leaves or chocolate shavings.

6. Enjoy:

- Enjoy these delightful Mint Chocolate Brownie Bites with their layers of rich brownie, refreshing mint, and decadent chocolate ganache!

Note:

- Adjust the amount of peppermint extract to your taste preference in the mint layer.
- Feel free to customize the appearance by adding sprinkles, crushed candy canes, or additional decorations on top.
- Store the brownie bites in the refrigerator if not serving immediately.

Honey Lavender Ice Cream

Ingredients:

For the Honey Lavender Base:

    2 cups heavy cream
    1 cup whole milk
    1/2 cup honey
    1-2 tablespoons culinary lavender buds (adjust to taste)
    1 teaspoon vanilla extract

For the Egg Custard:

    5 large egg yolks
    1/2 cup granulated sugar

Instructions:

1. Infuse the Cream:

a. Heat Cream and Milk:

- In a saucepan, combine heavy cream, whole milk, honey, and culinary lavender buds. Heat the mixture over medium heat until it just begins to simmer. Stir occasionally to dissolve the honey.

b. Steep Lavender:

- Once the mixture is warm, remove it from heat and let the lavender steep for about 15-20 minutes. Strain out the lavender buds using a fine-mesh sieve.

c. Add Vanilla:

- Stir in the vanilla extract and set aside.

2. Make the Egg Custard:

a. Whisk Egg Yolks and Sugar:

- In a bowl, whisk together the egg yolks and granulated sugar until the mixture becomes pale and slightly thickened.

b. Temper Eggs:

- Gradually pour a small amount of the warm lavender-infused cream into the egg yolk mixture, whisking constantly. This process, called tempering, prevents the eggs from curdling.

c. Combine Mixtures:

- Pour the tempered egg mixture back into the saucepan with the remaining lavender-infused cream. Cook over medium-low heat, stirring constantly, until the custard thickens enough to coat the back of a spoon.

d. Strain Custard:

- Strain the custard through a fine-mesh sieve into a clean bowl to remove any bits of cooked egg.

3. Chill and Freeze:

a. Cool and Refrigerate:

- Allow the custard to cool to room temperature. Cover the bowl with plastic wrap, ensuring it touches the surface of the custard to prevent a skin from forming. Refrigerate for at least 4 hours or overnight.

b. Churn in Ice Cream Maker:

- Once thoroughly chilled, churn the custard in an ice cream maker according to the manufacturer's instructions until it reaches a soft-serve consistency.

c. Transfer and Freeze:

- Transfer the churned ice cream to a lidded container, spreading it evenly. Freeze for at least 4 hours or overnight to achieve a firm texture.

4. Serve and Enjoy:

- Scoop the Honey Lavender Ice Cream into bowls or cones. Garnish with additional lavender buds or a drizzle of honey if desired. Enjoy the unique and delightful flavor of this homemade treat!

Notes:

- Adjust the amount of culinary lavender based on your taste preference. Start with a smaller amount and add more if needed.
- If you don't have an ice cream maker, you can pour the chilled custard into a lidded container and freeze it, stirring every 30 minutes until it reaches the desired consistency.

Raspberry Chocolate Tart

Ingredients:

For the Chocolate Crust:

    1 1/2 cups chocolate cookie crumbs (from about 20 chocolate sandwich cookies)
    1/3 cup unsalted butter, melted

For the Chocolate Ganache Filling:

    1 cup heavy cream
    8 ounces semi-sweet chocolate, finely chopped
    2 tablespoons unsalted butter
    1 teaspoon vanilla extract

For the Raspberry Topping:

    2 cups fresh raspberries
    2 tablespoons raspberry jam, melted

Optional Garnish:

    Whipped cream
    Chocolate shavings

Instructions:

1. Prepare the Chocolate Crust:

a. Crush Cookies:

- In a food processor, pulse the chocolate sandwich cookies until fine crumbs form.

b. Mix with Butter:

- Combine the cookie crumbs with melted butter in a bowl. Press the mixture into the bottom and up the sides of a tart pan with a removable bottom.

c. Chill:

- Place the crust in the refrigerator for at least 30 minutes to set.

2. Make the Chocolate Ganache Filling:

a. Heat Cream:

- In a saucepan, heat the heavy cream over medium heat until it just starts to simmer. Remove from heat.

b. Add Chocolate and Butter:

- Add the finely chopped semi-sweet chocolate and 2 tablespoons of butter to the hot cream. Let it sit for a minute, then stir until smooth and creamy.

c. Add Vanilla:

- Stir in the vanilla extract. Allow the ganache to cool slightly.

3. Assemble the Tart:

a. Pour Ganache:

- Pour the chocolate ganache into the prepared chocolate crust, spreading it evenly.

b. Chill:

- Place the tart in the refrigerator and let it set for at least 2 hours or until the ganache is firm.

4. Add Raspberry Topping:

a. Arrange Raspberries:

- Once the ganache is set, arrange fresh raspberries on top of the tart.

b. Glaze with Jam:

- Brush the raspberries with melted raspberry jam for a glossy finish.

5. Optional Garnish:

- Garnish the tart with whipped cream and chocolate shavings if desired.

6. Serve and Enjoy:

- Slice the Raspberry Chocolate Tart and serve chilled. Enjoy the rich and decadent combination of chocolate ganache and fresh raspberries!

Note:

- You can customize the tart by using different types of cookies for the crust or adding a layer of pastry cream or whipped ganache before arranging the raspberries.

Orange Creamsicle Cheesecake

Ingredients:

For the Crust:

    2 cups graham cracker crumbs
    1/2 cup unsalted butter, melted
    1/4 cup granulated sugar

For the Cheesecake Filling:

    4 packages (32 ounces total) cream cheese, softened
    1 cup granulated sugar
    4 large eggs
    1 teaspoon vanilla extract
    1/2 cup sour cream
    1/2 cup heavy cream

For the Orange Swirl:

    1/2 cup orange juice (freshly squeezed if possible)
    Zest of 1 orange
    1/4 cup granulated sugar

For the Orange Creamsicle Topping:

    1 cup heavy cream
    1/4 cup powdered sugar
    1 teaspoon vanilla extract
    Orange slices for garnish (optional)

Instructions:

1. Preheat the Oven:

- Preheat your oven to 325°F (163°C). Grease a 9-inch springform pan with butter or cooking spray.

2. Make the Crust:

a. Combine Ingredients:

- In a bowl, mix graham cracker crumbs, melted butter, and sugar until well combined.

b. Press into Pan:

- Press the mixture into the bottom of the prepared springform pan to form an even crust.

c. Bake:

- Bake the crust in the preheated oven for about 10 minutes. Remove from the oven and let it cool while you prepare the filling.

3. Make the Cheesecake Filling:

a. Beat Cream Cheese and Sugar:

- In a large mixing bowl, beat the softened cream cheese and sugar until smooth and creamy.

b. Add Eggs and Vanilla:

- Add the eggs one at a time, beating well after each addition. Mix in the vanilla extract.

c. Incorporate Sour Cream and Heavy Cream:

- Mix in the sour cream and heavy cream until the batter is smooth and well combined.

4. Make the Orange Swirl:

a. Combine Ingredients:

- In a small saucepan, combine orange juice, orange zest, and sugar. Heat over medium heat until the sugar dissolves and the mixture slightly thickens.

b. Cool:

- Let the orange swirl mixture cool to room temperature.

5. Assemble the Cheesecake:

a. Pour Batter:

- Pour the cream cheese filling over the cooled crust in the springform pan.

b. Add Orange Swirl:

- Drop spoonfuls of the cooled orange swirl mixture onto the cream cheese filling. Use a knife or skewer to create a swirl pattern.

6. Bake:

- Bake the cheesecake in the preheated oven for 50-60 minutes or until the edges are set, and the center is slightly jiggly.

7. Cool and Refrigerate:

- Allow the cheesecake to cool in the oven with the door ajar for about an hour, then refrigerate for at least 4 hours or overnight.

8. Make the Orange Creamsicle Topping:

a. Whip Cream:

- In a chilled bowl, whip the heavy cream, powdered sugar, and vanilla extract until stiff peaks form.

b. Spread on Cheesecake:

- Spread the whipped cream over the chilled cheesecake.

9. Garnish and Serve:

- Garnish with orange slices if desired. Slice and serve your delicious Orange Creamsicle Cheesecake!

Note:

- For a more intense orange flavor, you can add a few drops of orange extract to the orange swirl mixture or the cheesecake filling.
- Ensure that all ingredients for the cheesecake filling are at room temperature to achieve a smooth and creamy texture.

Berry Chia Seed Pudding

Ingredients:

For the Chia Seed Pudding:

    1/2 cup chia seeds
    2 cups almond milk (or any milk of your choice)
    2-3 tablespoons maple syrup or honey (adjust to taste)
    1 teaspoon vanilla extract

For the Berry Compote:

    1 cup mixed berries (strawberries, blueberries, raspberries)
    2 tablespoons maple syrup or honey
    1 tablespoon water
    1 teaspoon lemon juice

For Garnish (Optional):

    Fresh berries
    Sliced almonds or chopped nuts
    Mint leaves

Instructions:

1. Make the Chia Seed Pudding:

a. Combine Ingredients:

- In a bowl or jar, mix together chia seeds, almond milk, maple syrup (or honey), and vanilla extract.

b. Stir Well:

- Stir the mixture thoroughly, ensuring that the chia seeds are evenly distributed.

c. Refrigerate:

- Cover the bowl or jar and refrigerate for at least 4 hours or preferably overnight. Stir the mixture again after the first 30 minutes to prevent clumping.

2. Prepare the Berry Compote:

a. Cook Berries:

- In a saucepan, combine mixed berries, maple syrup (or honey), water, and lemon juice.

b. Simmer:

- Simmer the mixture over medium heat, stirring occasionally, until the berries break down and the mixture thickens to a compote consistency. This usually takes about 10-15 minutes.

c. Cool:

- Remove from heat and let the berry compote cool to room temperature.

3. Assemble the Berry Chia Seed Pudding:

a. Layer Pudding and Compote:

- Once the chia seed pudding has set, spoon a layer of it into serving glasses or jars.

b. Add Berry Compote:

- Top the chia seed pudding with a layer of the cooled berry compote.

c. Repeat Layers:

- Repeat the layers until the glasses are filled, finishing with a layer of berry compote on top.

4. Garnish (Optional):

- Garnish the Berry Chia Seed Pudding with fresh berries, sliced almonds or chopped nuts, and mint leaves for a burst of color and texture.

5. Serve and Enjoy:

- Serve the Berry Chia Seed Pudding chilled and enjoy a delightful and nutritious treat!

Variations:

- Yogurt Swirl: Add a layer of Greek yogurt between the chia seed pudding and berry compote for added creaminess.
- Citrus Zest: Enhance the flavor by adding a sprinkle of citrus zest (orange or lemon) to the chia seed pudding or on top as a garnish.
- Coconut Bliss: Use coconut milk for the chia seed pudding and top with toasted coconut flakes for a tropical twist.
- Granola Crunch: Sprinkle a layer of granola between the chia seed pudding and berry compote for a crunchy element.

This Berry Chia Seed Pudding is not only delicious but also packed with fiber, omega-3 fatty acids, and antioxidants. It makes for a satisfying and wholesome breakfast or a healthy dessert option.

Watermelon Sorbet

Ingredients:

    4 cups seedless watermelon, cubed
    1/2 cup granulated sugar
    2 tablespoons fresh lime juice
    1/4 cup water

Optional Garnish:

    Fresh mint leaves
    Lime slices

Instructions:

1. Prepare the Watermelon:

a. Remove Seeds:

- Ensure that the watermelon is seedless. If not, remove the seeds.

b. Cube Watermelon:

- Cut the watermelon into small cubes, measuring approximately 4 cups.

2. Make the Simple Syrup:

a. Combine Sugar and Water:

- In a small saucepan, combine the granulated sugar and water. Heat over medium heat, stirring occasionally, until the sugar completely dissolves. Remove from heat and let it cool.

b. Add Lime Juice:

- Stir in the fresh lime juice. Let the simple syrup with lime juice cool to room temperature.

3. Blend the Sorbet Mixture:

a. Blend Watermelon:

- In a blender or food processor, blend the cubed watermelon until smooth.

b. Strain (Optional):

- If desired, strain the watermelon puree through a fine-mesh sieve to remove any pulp. This step is optional, as some prefer the added texture.

c. Mix with Simple Syrup:

- In a large bowl, combine the watermelon puree with the cooled simple syrup and lime juice mixture. Mix well.

4. Chill:

- Place the mixture in the refrigerator and let it chill for at least 2 hours, ensuring it is well-cooled before transferring to the ice cream maker.

5. Churn in Ice Cream Maker:

- Pour the chilled watermelon mixture into an ice cream maker and churn according to the manufacturer's instructions until it reaches a soft-serve consistency.

6. Freeze:

- Transfer the churned sorbet into a lidded container and freeze for an additional 2-4 hours or until it firms up.

7. Serve:

- Scoop the Watermelon Sorbet into bowls or cones. Garnish with fresh mint leaves and lime slices if desired.

8. Enjoy:

- Enjoy the refreshing and fruity taste of homemade Watermelon Sorbet on a hot day!

Note:

- For a quicker version, you can pour the blended mixture into a shallow dish and freeze it. Every 30 minutes, stir the mixture with a fork to break up any ice crystals until it reaches the desired sorbet consistency.

Mango Coconut Popsicles

Ingredients:

    2 cups ripe mango, peeled and diced
    1 cup coconut milk (full-fat for creamier popsicles)
    1/4 cup honey or maple syrup (adjust to taste)
    1 teaspoon lime juice
    Shredded coconut (optional, for garnish)

Instructions:

1. Prepare Mango:

a. Peel and Dice Mango:

- Peel and dice ripe mango until you have approximately 2 cups.

2. Blend the Mixture:

a. Combine Ingredients:

- In a blender, combine the diced mango, coconut milk, honey (or maple syrup), and lime juice.

b. Blend until Smooth:

- Blend the ingredients until you achieve a smooth and creamy consistency.

3. Adjust Sweetness:

- Taste the mixture and adjust the sweetness by adding more honey or maple syrup if needed.

4. Fill Popsicle Molds:

a. Pour into Molds:

- Pour the mango coconut mixture into popsicle molds.

b. Optional: Add Shredded Coconut:

- If desired, sprinkle a bit of shredded coconut into each mold for added texture.

5. Freeze:

- Place the popsicle molds in the freezer and let them freeze for at least 4-6 hours or until completely set.

6. Unmold and Enjoy:

a. Run Mold Under Warm Water:

- To unmold the popsicles, run the bottom of the molds under warm water for a few seconds.

b. Remove Popsicles:

- Gently pull the popsicles out of the molds.

7. Serve and Enjoy:

- Serve the Mango Coconut Popsicles immediately and savor the tropical flavors!

Variations:

- Pineapple Twist: Add a cup of diced pineapple to the mixture for a tropical blend of mango and pineapple.
- Tropical Medley: Mix in other tropical fruits such as papaya or passion fruit for a diverse flavor profile.

- Creamier Texture: Increase the creaminess by incorporating a 1/2 cup of Greek yogurt or coconut cream into the mixture.
- Chia Seeds: For added texture and health benefits, stir in a tablespoon of chia seeds before pouring the mixture into the molds.

These Mango Coconut Popsicles are not only delicious but also a perfect way to cool down on a hot day. Enjoy the tropical goodness!

Lemon Raspberry Swirl Pound Cake

Ingredients:

For the Pound Cake:

    1 cup unsalted butter, softened
    2 cups granulated sugar
    4 large eggs
    3 cups all-purpose flour
    1/2 teaspoon baking powder
    1/2 teaspoon baking soda
    1/2 teaspoon salt
    1 cup sour cream
    2 teaspoons vanilla extract
    Zest of 2 lemons

For the Raspberry Swirl:

    1 cup fresh raspberries
    2 tablespoons granulated sugar

For the Lemon Glaze:

    1 cup powdered sugar
    2 tablespoons fresh lemon juice
    Lemon zest for garnish (optional)

Instructions:

1. Preheat the Oven:

- Preheat your oven to 325°F (163°C). Grease and flour a bundt pan.

2. Make the Raspberry Swirl:

a. Prepare Raspberries:

- In a small bowl, mash the fresh raspberries with a fork.

b. Add Sugar:

- Stir in the granulated sugar until well combined. Set aside.

3. Prepare the Pound Cake Batter:

a. Cream Butter and Sugar:

- In a large mixing bowl, cream together the softened butter and granulated sugar until light and fluffy.

b. Add Eggs:

- Add the eggs one at a time, beating well after each addition.

c. Combine Dry Ingredients:

- In a separate bowl, whisk together the flour, baking powder, baking soda, and salt.

d. Add Dry Ingredients to Batter:

- Gradually add the dry ingredients to the batter, alternating with the sour cream. Begin and end with the dry ingredients. Mix until just combined.

e. Add Vanilla and Lemon Zest:

- Mix in the vanilla extract and lemon zest until incorporated.

4. Layering and Swirling:

a. Fill the Bundt Pan:

- Spoon half of the pound cake batter into the prepared bundt pan, spreading it evenly.

b. Add Raspberry Swirl:

- Drop spoonfuls of the raspberry swirl mixture over the batter.

c. Swirl with a Knife:

- Use a knife to gently swirl the raspberry mixture into the batter.

d. Layer the Rest:

- Add the remaining pound cake batter on top of the raspberry swirl layer.

e. Swirl Again:

- Repeat the swirling process with the remaining raspberry mixture.

5. Bake:

- Bake in the preheated oven for approximately 60-70 minutes or until a toothpick inserted into the center comes out clean.

6. Cool:

a. Cool in Pan:

- Allow the pound cake to cool in the bundt pan for about 15 minutes.

b. Transfer to Rack:

- Carefully invert the cake onto a wire rack and let it cool completely.

7. Make the Lemon Glaze:

a. Whisk Ingredients:

- In a bowl, whisk together the powdered sugar and fresh lemon juice until smooth.

8. Glaze the Pound Cake:

- Drizzle the lemon glaze over the cooled pound cake.

9. Garnish (Optional):

- Garnish with additional lemon zest if desired.

10. Slice and Enjoy:

- Slice the Lemon Raspberry Swirl Pound Cake and enjoy the burst of citrus and berry flavors!

Note:

- Ensure the raspberries are well mashed for a smooth swirl in the cake.
- Adjust the sweetness of the glaze according to your preference by adding more or less powdered sugar.

Peach and Raspberry Crumble

Ingredients:

For the Fruit Filling:

> 4 cups fresh peaches, peeled and sliced
> 1 cup fresh raspberries
> 1/2 cup granulated sugar
> 2 tablespoons all-purpose flour
> 1 teaspoon vanilla extract
> 1 tablespoon lemon juice

For the Crumble Topping:

> 1 cup old-fashioned rolled oats
> 1/2 cup all-purpose flour
> 1/2 cup brown sugar, packed
> 1/2 teaspoon ground cinnamon
> 1/4 teaspoon salt
> 1/2 cup unsalted butter, cold and cut into small pieces

Optional Garnish:

> Vanilla ice cream or whipped cream

Instructions:

1. Preheat the Oven:

- Preheat your oven to 350°F (175°C). Grease a baking dish or individual ramekins.

2. Prepare the Fruit Filling:

a. Combine Ingredients:

- In a large mixing bowl, combine the sliced peaches, raspberries, granulated sugar, all-purpose flour, vanilla extract, and lemon juice. Toss until the fruit is evenly coated.

b. Let it Sit:

- Allow the fruit mixture to sit for about 10 minutes to let the flavors meld and release some juices.

3. Make the Crumble Topping:

a. Combine Dry Ingredients:

- In a separate bowl, combine the rolled oats, all-purpose flour, brown sugar, ground cinnamon, and salt.

b. Add Butter:

- Add the cold, diced butter to the dry ingredients.

c. Crumble Together:

- Using your fingers or a pastry cutter, crumble the butter into the dry ingredients until the mixture resembles coarse crumbs. Some larger clumps are okay for added texture.

4. Assemble the Crumble:

a. Layer Fruit Mixture:

- Spread the prepared fruit mixture evenly in the greased baking dish or ramekins.

b. Sprinkle Crumble Topping:

- Sprinkle the crumble topping over the fruit mixture, covering it evenly.

5. Bake:

- Bake in the preheated oven for 30-35 minutes or until the fruit is bubbling, and the crumble topping is golden brown.

6. Cool Slightly:

- Allow the peach and raspberry crumble to cool slightly before serving.

7. Serve:

- Serve the crumble warm, either on its own or with a scoop of vanilla ice cream or a dollop of whipped cream.

8. Enjoy:

- Enjoy the delightful combination of juicy peaches, tart raspberries, and the crisp crumble topping!

Note:

- Adjust the sugar quantity in the fruit filling based on the sweetness of your peaches and personal preference.
- You can use a mix of yellow and white peaches for a variety of flavors in the crumble.
- This recipe can be easily doubled for a larger crowd or for leftovers. Simply adjust the baking time accordingly.

Strawberry Basil Lemonade

Ingredients:

For the Strawberry Basil Syrup:

- 1 cup fresh strawberries, hulled and sliced
- 1/2 cup granulated sugar
- 1/2 cup water
- Handful of fresh basil leaves, torn

For the Lemonade:

- 1 cup fresh lemon juice (approximately 4-6 lemons)
- 4 cups cold water
- Ice cubes
- Fresh strawberries and basil leaves for garnish

Instructions:

1. Make the Strawberry Basil Syrup:

a. Combine Ingredients:

- In a saucepan, combine the sliced strawberries, granulated sugar, water, and torn basil leaves.

b. Bring to a Simmer:

- Heat the mixture over medium heat, stirring occasionally, until it comes to a simmer. Let it simmer for about 5-7 minutes, or until the strawberries are soft and the sugar is dissolved.

c. Mash and Strain:

- Mash the strawberries with a spoon while simmering. Afterward, strain the syrup through a fine-mesh sieve into a bowl, pressing on the solids to extract all the liquid. Discard the solids.

d. Cool:

- Let the strawberry basil syrup cool to room temperature.

2. Make the Lemonade:

a. Mix Lemon Juice and Water:

- In a pitcher, combine the fresh lemon juice and cold water.

b. Add Strawberry Basil Syrup:

- Pour the cooled strawberry basil syrup into the pitcher with the lemonade. Stir well to combine.

3. Serve:

a. Refrigerate:

- Refrigerate the strawberry basil lemonade for at least 1-2 hours to allow the flavors to meld.

b. Stir Before Serving:

- Before serving, stir the lemonade well. If it's too concentrated, you can dilute it with additional cold water.

4. Garnish and Enjoy:

- Pour the strawberry basil lemonade over ice cubes in glasses.
- Garnish each glass with fresh strawberry slices and basil leaves.

5. Serve Chilled and Enjoy:

- Serve the strawberry basil lemonade chilled and savor the refreshing combination of sweet strawberries, aromatic basil, and tangy lemon!

Variations:

- Sparkling Strawberry Basil Lemonade: Add a splash of sparkling water or club soda for a fizzy version.
- Minty Twist: Replace basil with fresh mint leaves for a strawberry mint lemonade.

- Berry Medley: Mix in other berries like blueberries or raspberries for a berry-infused lemonade.
- Sweetener Options: Adjust the sweetness by adding more or less sugar in the strawberry basil syrup according to your taste preference.

This Strawberry Basil Lemonade is perfect for a sunny day or as a delightful party beverage. It combines the sweetness of strawberries, the herbal notes of basil, and the zing of fresh lemons for a truly refreshing drink.

Blueberry Pancake Stack with Maple Syrup

Ingredients:

For the Blueberry Pancakes:

    2 cups all-purpose flour
    2 tablespoons granulated sugar
    1 tablespoon baking powder
    1/2 teaspoon salt
    2 large eggs
    1 1/2 cups milk
    1/4 cup unsalted butter, melted
    1 teaspoon vanilla extract
    1 cup fresh or frozen blueberries

For Serving:

    Maple syrup
    Additional blueberries for garnish
    Whipped cream (optional)
    Butter for serving (optional)

Instructions:

1. Make the Blueberry Pancake Batter:

a. Combine Dry Ingredients:

- In a large mixing bowl, whisk together the flour, sugar, baking powder, and salt.

b. Mix Wet Ingredients:

- In another bowl, beat the eggs and then add the milk, melted butter, and vanilla extract. Mix well.

c. Combine Wet and Dry Mixtures:

- Pour the wet ingredients into the dry ingredients and stir until just combined. Do not overmix; it's okay if there are a few lumps.

d. Fold in Blueberries:

- Gently fold in the blueberries into the pancake batter.

2. Cook the Blueberry Pancakes:

a. Preheat Griddle or Pan:

- Preheat a griddle or non-stick pan over medium heat. Lightly grease with butter or cooking spray.

b. Scoop Batter:

- Scoop 1/4 cup portions of the batter onto the griddle for each pancake.

c. Cook Until Bubbles Form:

- Cook until bubbles form on the surface of the pancakes and the edges look set.

d. Flip and Cook Other Side:

- Flip the pancakes and cook the other side until golden brown.

e. Repeat:

- Repeat until all the batter is used.

3. Assemble the Pancake Stack:

a. Stack the Pancakes:

- Stack the blueberry pancakes on a serving plate.

4. Serve:

a. Drizzle with Maple Syrup:

- Generously drizzle maple syrup over the pancake stack.

b. Garnish:

- Garnish with additional fresh blueberries on top.

c. Optional Extras:

- Add a dollop of whipped cream or a pat of butter on top if desired.

5. Enjoy:

- Serve the Blueberry Pancake Stack warm and enjoy a delightful breakfast or brunch!

Tips:

- For extra fluffiness, let the pancake batter rest for about 5-10 minutes before cooking.
- Keep pancakes warm by placing them in a preheated oven (around 200°F or 95°C) until ready to serve.
- Experiment with different toppings like sliced bananas, chopped nuts, or a sprinkle of powdered sugar for added variety.

Coconut Pineapple Cake

Ingredients:

For the Cake:

    2 cups all-purpose flour
    1 1/2 teaspoons baking powder
    1/2 teaspoon baking soda
    1/4 teaspoon salt
    1 cup unsalted butter, softened
    1 cup granulated sugar
    1 cup packed light brown sugar
    4 large eggs
    1 teaspoon vanilla extract
    1 cup canned crushed pineapple, drained
    1 cup shredded coconut (sweetened)

For the Coconut Cream Cheese Frosting:

    8 ounces cream cheese, softened
    1/2 cup unsalted butter, softened
    4 cups powdered sugar
    1 teaspoon vanilla extract
    1/2 cup shredded coconut (sweetened), for garnish

Instructions:

1. Preheat the Oven:

- Preheat your oven to 350°F (175°C). Grease and flour two 9-inch round cake pans.

2. Make the Cake:

a. Combine Dry Ingredients:

- In a bowl, whisk together the flour, baking powder, baking soda, and salt. Set aside.

b. Cream Butter and Sugars:

- In a large mixing bowl, cream together the softened butter, granulated sugar, and brown sugar until light and fluffy.

c. Add Eggs and Vanilla:

- Add the eggs one at a time, beating well after each addition. Mix in the vanilla extract.

d. Incorporate Dry Ingredients:

- Gradually add the dry ingredients to the wet ingredients, mixing just until combined.

e. Fold in Pineapple and Coconut:

- Gently fold in the drained crushed pineapple and shredded coconut until evenly distributed in the batter.

f. Divide Batter:

- Divide the batter evenly between the prepared cake pans.

3. Bake the Cake:

- Bake in the preheated oven for approximately 25-30 minutes or until a toothpick inserted into the center comes out clean.

4. Cool the Cake:

a. Cool in Pans:

- Allow the cakes to cool in the pans for about 10 minutes.

b. Transfer to Wire Rack:

- Transfer the cakes to a wire rack to cool completely.

5. Make the Coconut Cream Cheese Frosting:

a. Beat Cream Cheese and Butter:

- In a bowl, beat together the softened cream cheese and butter until smooth.

b. Add Powdered Sugar and Vanilla:

- Gradually add the powdered sugar, beating well after each addition. Mix in the vanilla extract.

6. Assemble the Cake:

a. Place Bottom Layer:

- Place one cake layer on a serving plate.

b. Frost Bottom Layer:

- Spread a layer of the coconut cream cheese frosting over the top of the first layer.

c. Add Top Layer:

- Place the second cake layer on top.

d. Frost Entire Cake:

- Frost the entire cake with the remaining coconut cream cheese frosting.

7. Garnish:

- Sprinkle shredded coconut over the top of the frosted cake for garnish.

8. Serve and Enjoy:

- Slice and serve the delicious Coconut Pineapple Cake. Enjoy the tropical flavors!

Note:

- If you want an extra burst of pineapple flavor, you can brush the cake layers with pineapple juice before frosting.
- Ensure the crushed pineapple is well-drained to prevent excess moisture in the cake batter.

Cherry Chocolate Chip Ice Cream Sandwiches

Ingredients:

For the Chocolate Chip Cookies:

- 1 cup unsalted butter, softened
- 1 cup granulated sugar
- 1 cup brown sugar, packed
- 2 large eggs
- 1 teaspoon vanilla extract
- 3 cups all-purpose flour
- 1 teaspoon baking powder
- 1/2 teaspoon baking soda
- 1/2 teaspoon salt
- 1 1/2 cups chocolate chips

For the Cherry Ice Cream:

- 2 cups fresh or frozen cherries, pitted and halved
- 1 cup granulated sugar
- 2 cups heavy cream
- 1 cup whole milk
- 1 teaspoon vanilla extract

Instructions:

1. Make the Chocolate Chip Cookies:

a. Preheat the Oven:

- Preheat your oven to 350°F (175°C). Line baking sheets with parchment paper.

b. Cream Butter and Sugars:

- In a large bowl, cream together the softened butter, granulated sugar, and brown sugar until smooth.

c. Add Eggs and Vanilla:

- Add the eggs one at a time, beating well after each addition. Mix in the vanilla extract.

d. Combine Dry Ingredients:

- In a separate bowl, whisk together the flour, baking powder, baking soda, and salt.

e. Add Dry Ingredients to Wet:

- Gradually add the dry ingredients to the wet ingredients, mixing until just combined.

f. Fold in Chocolate Chips:

- Gently fold in the chocolate chips until evenly distributed in the cookie dough.

g. Scoop Dough:

- Using a cookie scoop or tablespoon, drop rounded portions of dough onto the prepared baking sheets.

h. Bake:

- Bake in the preheated oven for 10-12 minutes or until the edges are golden brown. Allow the cookies to cool completely.

2. Make the Cherry Ice Cream:

a. Prepare Cherries:

- If using fresh cherries, pit and halve them. If using frozen cherries, let them thaw slightly.

b. Cook Cherries:

- In a saucepan, combine the cherries and granulated sugar. Cook over medium heat, stirring occasionally, until the cherries release their juices and the sugar is dissolved. This takes about 8-10 minutes.

c. Cool:

- Remove from heat and let the cherry mixture cool to room temperature.

d. Blend Cherry Mixture:

- Puree the cooled cherry mixture in a blender or food processor until smooth.

e. Mix with Cream and Milk:

- In a mixing bowl, combine the cherry puree, heavy cream, whole milk, and vanilla extract. Mix well.

f. Chill:

- Refrigerate the ice cream mixture for at least 4 hours or overnight to chill.

g. Churn in Ice Cream Maker:

- Pour the chilled cherry ice cream mixture into an ice cream maker and churn according to the manufacturer's instructions until it reaches a soft-serve consistency.

h. Layer in Container:

- In a lidded container, alternate layers of churned cherry ice cream and crumbled chocolate chip cookies. Swirl gently to combine.

i. Freeze:

- Freeze the ice cream for an additional 4-6 hours or until it's firm.

3. Assemble the Ice Cream Sandwiches:

a. Prepare Cookies:

- Once the ice cream is fully frozen, scoop a portion onto the flat side of a chocolate chip cookie.

b. Top with Another Cookie:

- Place another chocolate chip cookie, flat side down, on top of the ice cream, creating a sandwich.

c. Press Gently:

- Press the cookies together gently to adhere.

d. Optional: Roll in Toppings:

- If desired, roll the exposed ice cream edge in additional chocolate chips or sprinkles for a decorative touch.

4. Freeze and Serve:

- Place the assembled ice cream sandwiches on a baking sheet and freeze for at least 2 hours or until the ice cream is firm.
- Serve and enjoy these delicious Cherry Chocolate Chip Ice Cream Sandwiches!

Note:

- You can customize these ice cream sandwiches by rolling the edges in chopped nuts, coconut flakes, or crushed cookies for added texture and flavor.

Lemon Thyme Shortbread Cookies

Ingredients:

    1 cup unsalted butter, softened
    1/2 cup powdered sugar
    1 tablespoon fresh thyme leaves, finely chopped
    Zest of 1 lemon
    2 cups all-purpose flour
    1/4 teaspoon salt
    Additional powdered sugar for dusting (optional)

Instructions:

1. Preheat the Oven:

- Preheat your oven to 350°F (175°C). Line a baking sheet with parchment paper.

2. Prepare the Thyme:

- Finely chop the fresh thyme leaves.

3. Cream Butter and Sugar:

a. Beat Together:

- In a large bowl, beat together the softened butter and powdered sugar until creamy and well combined.

b. Add Thyme and Lemon Zest:

- Add the finely chopped thyme leaves and lemon zest to the butter-sugar mixture. Beat until the thyme and lemon zest are evenly distributed.

4. Mix Dry Ingredients:

a. Combine Flour and Salt:

- In a separate bowl, whisk together the all-purpose flour and salt.

b. Add to Butter Mixture:

- Gradually add the flour mixture to the butter mixture, mixing until a soft dough forms.

5. Shape the Cookies:

a. Roll Dough into Log:

- Shape the dough into a log, approximately 2 inches in diameter.

b. Chill Dough:

- Wrap the log of dough in plastic wrap and refrigerate for at least 1 hour or until firm.

6. Slice and Bake:

a. Preheat Oven:

- Remove the chilled dough from the refrigerator and let it sit for a few minutes. Preheat the oven to 350°F (175°C) if it's not already preheated.

b. Slice Cookies:

- Slice the dough into rounds, about 1/4 to 1/2 inch thick, and place them on the prepared baking sheet.

c. Bake:

- Bake in the preheated oven for 12-15 minutes or until the edges are lightly golden.

7. Cool:

- Allow the cookies to cool on the baking sheet for a few minutes before transferring them to a wire rack to cool completely.

8. Optional Dusting:

- Dust the cooled cookies with powdered sugar if desired for a decorative touch.

9. Serve and Enjoy:

- Serve these delightful Lemon Thyme Shortbread Cookies with your favorite tea or coffee. Enjoy the unique combination of citrusy lemon, aromatic thyme, and buttery shortbread!

Note:

- Make sure to use fresh thyme leaves for the best flavor. If you don't have fresh thyme, you can substitute with dried thyme, but adjust the quantity accordingly.
- Experiment with the thickness of the cookie slices to achieve your desired level of crispiness. Thinner slices will result in a crisper cookie, while thicker slices will be more tender.

Raspberry Almond Tart

Ingredients:

For the Almond Tart Crust:

- 1 cup all-purpose flour
- 1/2 cup almond flour
- 1/4 cup granulated sugar
- 1/2 cup unsalted butter, chilled and diced
- 1 large egg yolk
- 1 tablespoon ice water (as needed)

For the Almond Frangipane Filling:

- 1/2 cup unsalted butter, softened
- 1/2 cup granulated sugar
- 1 cup almond flour
- 2 large eggs
- 1 teaspoon almond extract
- 1/4 teaspoon salt

For Topping:

- Fresh raspberries
- Raspberry jam or apricot jam (for glazing)

Instructions:

1. Prepare the Almond Tart Crust:

a. Combine Dry Ingredients:

- In a food processor, pulse together the all-purpose flour, almond flour, and granulated sugar.

b. Add Butter:

- Add the chilled, diced butter and pulse until the mixture resembles coarse crumbs.

c. Add Egg Yolk:

- Add the egg yolk and pulse until the dough starts to come together.

d. Add Ice Water:

- If needed, add ice water, one tablespoon at a time, until the dough forms a ball.

e. Chill Dough:

- Shape the dough into a disk, wrap it in plastic wrap, and refrigerate for at least 30 minutes.

2. Preheat the Oven:

- Preheat your oven to 375°F (190°C). Grease and flour a tart pan.

3. Roll Out and Fit the Crust:

a. Roll Out Dough:

- On a floured surface, roll out the chilled dough to fit your tart pan.

b. Fit into Tart Pan:

- Carefully transfer the rolled-out dough to the tart pan, press it into the bottom and sides, and trim any excess.

c. Prick with Fork:

- Prick the bottom of the crust with a fork to prevent it from puffing up during baking.

4. Bake the Crust:

- Bake the tart crust in the preheated oven for 15-18 minutes or until it turns golden. Let it cool completely.

5. Prepare the Almond Frangipane Filling:

a. Cream Butter and Sugar:

- In a bowl, cream together the softened butter and granulated sugar until light and fluffy.

b. Add Almond Flour:

- Add the almond flour and mix until well combined.

c. Add Eggs and Flavoring:

- Add the eggs one at a time, mixing well after each addition. Stir in the almond extract and salt.

6. Assemble and Bake:

a. Spread Frangipane in Crust:

- Spread the almond frangipane filling evenly over the cooled tart crust.

b. Bake Again:

- Bake in the preheated oven for 20-25 minutes or until the filling is set and golden brown.

7. Decorate with Raspberries:

- Once the tart has cooled, arrange fresh raspberries on top.

8. Glaze with Jam:

- Warm some raspberry or apricot jam and gently brush it over the raspberries for a glossy finish.

9. Chill and Serve:

- Chill the tart in the refrigerator for at least an hour before slicing. Serve and enjoy your Raspberry Almond Tart!

Note:

- Feel free to customize the fruit topping based on what's in season or your personal preferences. You can use other berries or a mix of fruits for variation.
- This tart can be served with a dusting of powdered sugar for added sweetness and presentation.

Peach Bellini Pops

Ingredients:

    2 cups ripe peaches, peeled and sliced
    1/4 cup granulated sugar (adjust to taste)
    1 tablespoon lemon juice
    1 cup Prosecco or sparkling wine
    1/4 cup peach schnapps (optional)
    Fresh mint leaves for garnish (optional)

Instructions:

1. Prepare the Peach Mixture:

a. Peel and Slice Peaches:

- Peel and slice ripe peaches until you have approximately 2 cups.

b. Blend Peaches:

- In a blender or food processor, blend the peaches until smooth.

c. Add Sugar and Lemon Juice:

- Add granulated sugar and lemon juice to the blended peaches. Blend again until the sugar is dissolved.

2. Combine with Sparkling Ingredients:

a. Add Prosecco and Peach Schnapps:

- Pour the blended peach mixture into a bowl. Add Prosecco and peach schnapps (if using). Stir gently to combine.

b. Taste and Adjust:

- Taste the mixture and adjust the sweetness by adding more sugar if needed.

3. Fill Popsicle Molds:

a. Pour into Molds:

- Pour the peach Bellini mixture into popsicle molds.

b. Optional: Add Mint Leaves:

- If desired, add fresh mint leaves to each mold for a burst of freshness.

4. Freeze:

- Place the popsicle molds in the freezer and let them freeze for at least 4-6 hours or until completely set.

5. Unmold and Serve:

a. Run Mold Under Warm Water:

- To unmold the popsicles, run the bottom of the molds under warm water for a few seconds.

b. Remove Popsicles:

- Gently pull the popsicles out of the molds.

6. Serve and Enjoy:

- Serve these delightful Peach Bellini Popsicles on a hot day or as a refreshing treat for any occasion.

Note:

- Adjust the amount of Prosecco and peach schnapps based on your preference for alcohol content.
- For a non-alcoholic version, you can replace the Prosecco and peach schnapps with sparkling water or peach nectar.
- Experiment with different molds and shapes to add a fun touch to your Peach Bellini Popsicles.

Blueberry Cheesecake Ice Cream

Ingredients:

For the Blueberry Swirl:

    1 cup fresh or frozen blueberries
    2 tablespoons granulated sugar
    1 tablespoon lemon juice

For the Cheesecake Ice Cream Base:

    2 cups heavy cream
    1 cup whole milk
    1 cup granulated sugar
    8 ounces cream cheese, softened
    1 teaspoon vanilla extract
    1 cup graham cracker crumbs

Instructions:

1. Prepare the Blueberry Swirl:

a. Cook Blueberries:

- In a small saucepan over medium heat, combine blueberries, sugar, and lemon juice. Cook until the blueberries burst and release their juices, stirring occasionally. Simmer for about 5-7 minutes until the mixture thickens. Remove from heat and let it cool.

b. Blend or Mash:

- You can either blend the blueberry mixture for a smooth swirl or mash it with a fork for a chunkier texture. Set aside to cool completely.

2. Make the Cheesecake Ice Cream Base:

a. Soften Cream Cheese:

- In a mixing bowl, beat the softened cream cheese until smooth.

b. Add Sugar and Vanilla:

- Add granulated sugar and vanilla extract to the cream cheese, and beat until well combined.

c. Incorporate Cream and Milk:

- Gradually add the heavy cream and whole milk, mixing until the mixture is smooth and well incorporated.

d. Chill Mixture:

- Cover the bowl and refrigerate the ice cream base for at least 4 hours or overnight to chill thoroughly.

3. Churn the Ice Cream:

- Pour the chilled ice cream base into your ice cream maker and churn according to the manufacturer's instructions until it reaches a soft-serve consistency.

4. Layer and Swirl:

a. Layer in Container:

- In a storage container, layer the churned cheesecake ice cream with spoonfuls of the blueberry swirl.

b. Swirl with a Knife:

- Use a knife to gently swirl the blueberry mixture into the ice cream, creating a marbled effect.

5. Freeze:

- Freeze the blueberry cheesecake ice cream for at least 4-6 hours or until it reaches your desired firmness.

6. Serve and Enjoy:

- Scoop the Blueberry Cheesecake Ice Cream into bowls or cones. Enjoy the delicious combination of creamy cheesecake ice cream with swirls of sweet and tangy blueberry!

Optional:

- Garnish with additional graham cracker crumbs or fresh blueberries when serving.
- Drizzle extra blueberry sauce on top for added flavor.

This homemade Blueberry Cheesecake Ice Cream is a delightful treat, combining the richness of cheesecake with the sweetness of blueberry swirls. Perfect for a summer indulgence!

Orange Creamsicle Cupcakes

Ingredients:

For the Cupcakes:

    1 3/4 cups all-purpose flour
    1 teaspoon baking powder
    1/2 teaspoon baking soda
    1/4 teaspoon salt
    1/2 cup unsalted butter, softened
    1 cup granulated sugar
    2 large eggs
    2 teaspoons orange zest
    1/3 cup fresh orange juice
    1/2 cup buttermilk
    1 teaspoon vanilla extract

For the Orange Creamsicle Frosting:

    1/2 cup unsalted butter, softened
    2 cups powdered sugar
    2 tablespoons fresh orange juice
    1 teaspoon vanilla extract
    Orange food coloring (optional)
    Orange zest for garnish (optional)

Instructions:

1. Preheat the Oven:

- Preheat your oven to 350°F (175°C). Line a muffin tin with cupcake liners.

2. Make the Cupcakes:

a. Combine Dry Ingredients:

- In a bowl, whisk together the flour, baking powder, baking soda, and salt. Set aside.

b. Cream Butter and Sugar:

- In a large bowl, cream together the softened butter and granulated sugar until light and fluffy.

c. Add Eggs and Orange Zest:

- Add the eggs one at a time, beating well after each addition. Mix in the orange zest.

d. Mix in Dry Ingredients:

- Gradually add the dry ingredients to the wet ingredients, alternating with the fresh orange juice. Begin and end with the dry ingredients.

e. Add Buttermilk and Vanilla:

- Mix in the buttermilk and vanilla extract until the batter is smooth.

3. Fill Cupcake Liners:

- Divide the batter evenly among the cupcake liners, filling each about 2/3 full.

4. Bake:

- Bake in the preheated oven for 18-20 minutes or until a toothpick inserted into the center comes out clean.

5. Make the Orange Creamsicle Frosting:

a. Beat Butter:

- In a separate bowl, beat the softened butter until creamy.

b. Add Powdered Sugar:

- Gradually add the powdered sugar, beating well after each addition.

c. Add Orange Juice and Vanilla:

- Mix in the fresh orange juice and vanilla extract until the frosting is smooth and fluffy.

d. Adjust Color (Optional):

- If desired, add orange food coloring to achieve a creamsicle color.

6. Frost the Cupcakes:

- Once the cupcakes are completely cooled, frost them with the orange creamsicle frosting using a piping bag or spatula.

7. Garnish (Optional):

- Garnish with additional orange zest for a burst of citrus flavor.

8. Serve and Enjoy:

- Serve these delightful Orange Creamsicle Cupcakes and enjoy the sweet and tangy combination reminiscent of the classic creamsicle treat!

Note:

- For an extra citrus kick, you can add a small amount of orange extract to the cupcake batter or frosting.
- Adjust the sweetness of the frosting by adding more or less powdered sugar according to your taste preference.

Mint Chocolate Mousse

Ingredients:

For the Chocolate Mousse:

    200g (7 oz) high-quality dark chocolate, chopped
    1/4 cup unsalted butter
    1/4 cup sugar
    1 teaspoon pure vanilla extract
    1 1/2 cups heavy cream, chilled

For the Mint Whipped Cream:

    1 cup heavy cream, chilled
    1/4 cup powdered sugar
    1/2 teaspoon peppermint extract (adjust to taste)
    Green food coloring (optional)

For Garnish:

    Grated chocolate or chocolate shavings
    Fresh mint leaves

Instructions:

1. Prepare the Chocolate Mousse:

a. Melt Chocolate and Butter:

- In a heatproof bowl, melt the chopped dark chocolate and butter together over a double boiler or in the microwave. Stir until smooth.

b. Add Sugar and Vanilla:

- Stir in the sugar and vanilla extract until well combined.

c. Let it Cool:

- Allow the chocolate mixture to cool to room temperature.

d. Whip Heavy Cream:

- In a separate bowl, whip the chilled heavy cream until stiff peaks form.

e. Combine and Fold:

- Gently fold the whipped cream into the cooled chocolate mixture until smooth and well combined. Be gentle to maintain the mousse's light texture.

f. Chill:

- Divide the chocolate mousse into serving glasses or bowls and refrigerate for at least 2 hours to set.

2. Make the Mint Whipped Cream:

a. Whip Heavy Cream:

- In a chilled bowl, whip the heavy cream until it begins to thicken.

b. Add Powdered Sugar and Mint Extract:

- Gradually add the powdered sugar and peppermint extract to the whipped cream. Whip until stiff peaks form.

c. Optional: Add Food Coloring:

- If desired, add a few drops of green food coloring to achieve a minty color.

3. Assemble and Garnish:

a. Top with Mint Whipped Cream:

- Spoon or pipe the mint whipped cream on top of the set chocolate mousse.

b. Garnish:

- Garnish with grated chocolate or chocolate shavings and fresh mint leaves.

4. Serve and Enjoy:

- Serve the Mint Chocolate Mousse immediately or refrigerate until ready to serve. Enjoy the delightful combination of rich chocolate and refreshing mint!

Note:

- Adjust the peppermint extract to your taste preference. Start with a small amount and add more if needed.
- Feel free to experiment with different garnishes like crushed peppermint candies or a drizzle of chocolate sauce for added decadence.

Vanilla Berry Popsicles

Ingredients:

    1 cup mixed berries (strawberries, blueberries, raspberries)
    1 tablespoon honey or maple syrup
    1 teaspoon lemon juice
    1 teaspoon vanilla extract
    2 cups vanilla yogurt (Greek or regular)
    Popsicle molds and sticks

Instructions:

1. Prepare the Berry Puree:

a. Blend Berries:

- In a blender or food processor, combine the mixed berries, honey or maple syrup, and lemon juice. Blend until you achieve a smooth puree.

b. Strain (Optional):

- If you prefer a smoother texture, you can strain the berry puree through a fine-mesh sieve to remove seeds. This step is optional.

2. Mix with Vanilla Yogurt:

a. Combine with Vanilla Yogurt:

- In a bowl, mix the berry puree with vanilla extract into the vanilla yogurt. Stir until well combined.

b. Adjust Sweetness:

- Taste the mixture and adjust the sweetness by adding more honey or maple syrup if needed.

3. Fill Popsicle Molds:

a. Layer the Mixture:

- Spoon the berry and vanilla yogurt mixture into popsicle molds, layering it with alternating spoonfuls to create a swirled effect.

b. Tap to Remove Air Bubbles:

- Tap the molds on the counter to remove any air bubbles and help the mixture settle.

c. Insert Sticks:

- Insert popsicle sticks into the center of each mold.

4. Freeze:

- Place the popsicle molds in the freezer and let them freeze for at least 4-6 hours or until fully set.

5. Unmold and Enjoy:

a. Run Mold Under Warm Water:

- To unmold the popsicles, run the bottom of the molds under warm water for a few seconds.

b. Remove Popsicles:

- Gently pull the popsicles out of the molds.

6. Serve and Enjoy:

- Serve these refreshing Vanilla Berry Popsicles on a hot day or as a delightful treat for both kids and adults.

Note:

- Feel free to customize the berry mixture with your favorite combination of fruits.
- For added texture, you can stir in additional whole berries into the yogurt mixture before filling the molds.
- Experiment with different types of yogurt, such as Greek yogurt for a creamier texture or non-dairy alternatives for a vegan version.